CONTEN

FOREWORD

This is the first in a series of booklets designed to accompany the report **Community and ethnic relations in Europe**, published by the Council of Europe in 1991[1]. *By community relations* is meant all aspects of the relations between migrants or ethnic groups of immigrant origin and the host society, and the report sets out proposals for a comprehensive approach to community relations policy in the Organisation's member States[2].

Following on from its work on community relations, the European Committee on Migration (CDMG) has now embarked on a new project entitled: *The integration of immigrants: towards equal opportunities*. This project aims to promote the exchange of practical experience between people who are attempting, in a variety of different ways, to put the community relations approach into practice.

The present booklet is the outcome of a meeting held in Strasbourg in September 1992 on the theme of *police training concerning migrants and ethnic relations*.

A consultant, Dr. Robin Oakley of the Specialist Support Unit (United Kingdom), played a leading part in the preparation of this meeting and in the follow-up to it. The participants at the meeting included the persons responsible for the main initiatives under way in the member States to introduce community and ethnic relations perspectives into police training; a number of officials with policy-making responsibilities

---

[1]   It can be ordered under the reference MG-CR (91) 1 final E.

[2]   These number 32 at present: Austria, Belgium, Bulgaria, Cyprus, Czech Republic, Denmark, Estonia, Finland, France, Germany, Greece, Hungary, Iceland, Ireland, Italy, Liechtenstein, Lithuania, Luxembourg, Malta, Netherlands, Norway, Poland, Portugal, Romania, San Marino, Slovak Republic, Slovenia, Spain, Sweden, Switzerland, Turkey, United Kingdom.

in the field of police training also took part. The full list of participants is given at the end of the booklet: this will enable readers who so wish to make contact with those responsible for the various training initiatives.

The first part of the booklet comprises the *Practical Guidelines*, a document drawn up by the consultant on the basis of the conclusions agreed upon at the meeting. In the hope that they will be of service to others wishing to introduce an awareness of immigration and community relations issues into police training, these guidelines are commended to the attention of all these responsible for police training in European countries.

For those wishing to know more about the initiatives presented at the meeting, there follows a series of shortened versions of the case-study papers which were prepared by those responsible. The full original versions of these papers can be obtained from the Secretariat in Strasbourg.

In addition, as part of the preparation for the meeting, the consultant conducted a questionnaire survey designed to discover the extent and nature of the training being provided in European countries to assist police officers to deal with matters concerning migrants and ethnic relations. The results of this survey are also set out in the booklet.

Interest in these aspects of police training is continuing to grow. It is likely that new experiments have started which are not covered by the questionnaire survey and that the case-studies presented at the meeting are no longer fully up to date. We would be glad to hear from readers about new developments. We would also encourage users of this booklet to let us have their observations on the practical guidelines.

Finally, I should like to take this opportunity of thanking the consultant, Dr. Robin Oakley, for all he has done to make this work possible. Thanks are also due to all those who took part in the meeting, especially those whose written contributions are summarised here.

Robin Guthrie
Director of Social
and Economic Affairs
Council of Europe

PRACTICAL

GUIDELINES

Introduction

This document sets out practical guidelines for those with responsibility for the training of police officers on matters concerning migrants and ethnic relations.

The practical guidelines are based upon existing experience in police training in a number of European countries. This experience was identified and brought together in a Meeting of Experts organised by the Council of Europe in September 1992. A Europe-wide questionnaire survey of current practice in addressing issues concerning migrants and ethnic relations in police training was carried out in preparation for the meeting. Experts from ten countries then presented detailed accounts of current training programmes at the meeting itself. The report of the survey, the papers prepared by the experts, and the conclusions of the meeting are all available separately.

The practical guidelines which follow have been drawn up subsequently by the consultant who has assisted the Council of Europe with this particular meeting. They have been designed to distil from the experience reported to that meeting those lessons which will be most useful to others, especially in countries where there has been little previous experience of addressing issues concerning migrants and ethnic relations in police training.

The phrase "migrants and ethnic relations" has been employed to delineate generally the scope of the guidelines. it is recognised that not all countries use the same terminology. By "migrants" should be understood all resident ethnic or racial groups of immigrant origin, including refugee groups. By "ethnic relations" should be understood all relations between such groups, including racism and xenophobia, and especially their manifestations in the form of violence and harassment of minorities.

Context

During recent decades, Europe has entered a new and unprecedented phase in its history so far as the movement and composition of population is concerned. It is important to identify the precise nature of this change since it is the context in which the need for guidelines of this kind has arisen.

Racially and culturally the population of Europe has remained relatively stable and homogenous over many centuries. The Christian religion, albeit in various denominational forms, has been culturally dominant for more than a millennium. The spread of Islam into Europe was resisted during the Middle Ages, and Jewish communities (despite the claims of anti-semitic ideologies) have remained small and in most respects marginal in the territories in which they have been able to settle. Population movement, apart from internal migration, has been almost exclusively outward - oriented until very recently - chiefly during the 19th and early 20th centuries to the Americas and to other European colonial domains. Europe's connection with the indigenous populations of these continents has been a distant one, structured for the most part by relations of cultural and political domination and rationalised by theories of racial and cultural superiority.

The aftermath of the 1939-45 war brought a transformation to this situation in Europe. Demographic and economic changes affecting mainly the industrialised north produced a demand for labour that was only partially met by internal migration from the Mediterranean Basin. The collapse of the colonial political and economic framework, the search for means of economic livelihood throughout the Third World, the opening up of new opportunities for transport and communication, and the possibility for colonial citizens of entry into the territories of their European "masters" - all these factors combined to produce an immigration into Europe of settlers of ethnic and racial origins quite new to the European tradition. These movements may have affected some European countries more than - or earlier than - others. However, it is an undeniable fact that *all* countries have become or are beginning to become involved in what is a permanent and irreversible process of Europe-wide social and cultural change. Europe as a whole, due to forces arising directly out of its own role in world history, is increasingly becoming a multi-racial, multi-cultural society.

Europe has yet to come to terms with the reality of this change and with its implications. In the first place the process is a complex one, affecting different countries in different ways. Moreover, economically-driven migration has now been supplemented by a politically-driven movement of refugees and asylum-seekers towards the relative freedom and safety of Europe. Economic decline and unemployment within the countries of immigration have provoked resentment and hostility among the indigenous population towards visible minorities perceived to be competing for jobs and housing. Xenophobic and racial violence, often perpetrated or at least encouraged by extremist right-wing nationalist groups, has erupted dramatically across Europe within the past few years (European Parliament 1990, Oakley 1992). Progress towards integration and equal treatment for communities of migrant origin has been slow at best, and is subject to many kinds of obstacles and resistance.

Public service agencies such as the police have important responsibilities in this situation. In the first place, where acts of a racist or xenophobic nature contravene the criminal law, it is the responsibility of the police to deal with such incidents, to help to prevent them, and to give protection to victimised communities. Secondly, the police like other public service agencies must ensure that their treatment of members of migrant and minority ethnic communities is fair, in accordance with human rights, and in general is of the same high standard as towards all other sections of the community. They must ensure that no prejudice or ethnocentrism obstructs equitable treatment, and that there is the same level of understanding of the culture and background of the minority communities (as well as sensitivity towards any special needs) as there is with regard to the majority group. All police forces need to meet this relatively new challenge arising from Europe's transformation from a mono-ethnic society into a multi-ethnic one. The transformation must be reflected in the staffing, internal ethos, and quality of external service delivery of every European police force, just as it must in all other kinds of public service agency. Although some progress has been made in this direction in certain countries, on the whole progress is slow in pace and still limited in scale, and there remains a substantial challenge ahead. Training programmes have an important role to play in helping to meet this challenge.

The role of training

In any public service organisation, training will play a major part in ensuring that officers possess the necessary knowledge, skills and attitudes to conduct themselves in a professional manner and to perform their roles effectively and in accordance with the policy of the organisation. Most police forces in Europe devote a very substantial amount of time both to initial and in-service training to achieve these goals.

-       *Initial and In-Service Training*

The inclusion of matters concerning migrants and ethnic relations is essential in both initial and in-service training for police officers. In initial training, police recruits will need to be prepared for carrying out their role in a multi-cultural, multi-racial environment, and for implementing any laws or policies which specifically relate to migrant or ethnic issues. In in-service training, officers will need to develop their capacities further, especially by reflecting on and thus learning from their previous professional experiences relating to such matters. They may also need to be briefed on recent developments concerning migrants and ethnic relations that are of relevance to their work, and to consider the implications of migrant and ethnic issues when undergoing training for a change of rank or role. In addition, for officers who have not received the initial training referred to above, it will be necessary to provide "catch-up" training along the same lines, in the form of a programme of special in-service provision for all serving officers.

- *Training alone cannot achieve change*

Effective training should be able to achieve the appropriate standards of knowledge, attitude and skill in these areas, but training alone cannot guarantee that the behaviour of which the trainee should now be capable will necessarily be carried out. Many other factors intervene to influence whether or not this will be the case. Research into the effectiveness of police training on these issues has persistently shown that positive training effects tend to be weakened or negated when the trainee returns to the work environment. Negative experiences on the job, pressure from peers, and lack of management commitment and support all commonly conspire to ensure that the change intended to be introduced through training does not come about. On racial and ethnic issues, such resistance may sometimes be strong on account of the cynicism and elements of racism and xenophobia that can become embedded in everyday police culture.

- *Training requires organisational support*

Training alone should not be expected to achieved the desired organisational goals, any more in this subject area than in any other field of police training. The immediate effects of training must be supported by management in the workplace - by leadership, by supervision, by rewards and sanctions, and by promotion of high standards of professionalism generally. However, the goal should not simply be one of changing the knowledge, attitudes and skills of individuals. The goal rather should be one of achieving change at the organisational level, so that police ethics, staffing, and mode of operation and service provision reflect today's multi-racial, multi-cultural society.

- *Need for organisational commitment*

Before introducing a training programme on matters relating to migrants and ethnic relations any police organisation should, therefore, be clearly and publicly committed to the changes which the training is intended to help bring about. Without such organisational commitment at policy level, even well-conceived training initiatives will have limited impact on account of lack of organisational support. For example, this was one of the reasons for the failure of the first national training initiative in this field in Britain during the 1980s. The programme of work of the present "Specialist Support Unit" now takes this factor fully into account (see sections I.11; I.12 and I.13 below).

- *Need for strategy for organisational change*

In addition there should be a defined strategy for achieving these changes, and the specific role of training within this strategy should be clearly identified. The *Positive Action Plan for Police and Minorities* introduced by the Dutch Government in 1988 provides an example of this approach (see sections I.7; I.8 and I.13 below). Training is one of four components in the Dutch strategy, which as a whole is designed to transform the Dutch police service from a mono-ethnic into a multi-ethnic organisation.

- *A top-down process*

In view of the generally hierarchical nature of police organisations, the process of change will need to begin "at the top". Training will therefore have a key role to play at the very outset of the change process. This initial role will be to enable senior managers and policy-makers to identify the challenge to the organisation of issues concerning migrants and ethnic relations, and to formulate a strategic policy response. The "Indian Summer Course" at the Police Study Centre at Warnsveld in the Netherlands provides an example of a training course for senior officers hich has been designed for this purpose, and thus to initiate a change process throughout the Dutch police system nationally (see section I.7 below).

The role of recruitment

Alongside training, the recruitment of persons of migrant or minority ethnic origin must also play an important role in the type of wider strategy for organisational change referred to above. The composition of the staff of the police (like that of any public service agency) should be expected normally to reflect the composition of the community it serves. This will help to create confidence in the police among all sections of the community; it will also help to promote understanding, respect and sensitivity towards minority groups within the everyday culture of the police. In the Netherlands, recruitment is seen as of central importance for these reasons.

-       *Recruitment alone will not produce change*

However, once again, recruitment alone should not be relied on to achieve these goals, for two reasons. Firstly, experience in Britain and other countries suggests that recruitment from minority ethnic groups is likely to be a slow process. In many countries, nationality laws restrict entry into the police, and members of minority ethnic groups often do not see a police   career as attractive. Secondly, those who come forward as recruits may not be typical members of their communities, and they will come under strong peer pressure to conform to traditional police ways. Moreover, their aspiration will be to become professional police officers not community mediators, and they should not be treated as the latter unless they choose to take up specialist posts of this kind. These points are well demonstrated in a study of black police officers in New York City (see Leinen 1984).

- *Training for recruitment and retention*

Training, however, will play an important role in increasing the recruitment and retention of officers of migrant and minority ethnic origin. Training for staff of the organisation will be needed to contribute in three ways. First, training will be needed for officers responsible for recruitment and selection: to ensure no direct or indirect racial discrimination takes place, and to generally promote equal opportunity principles in the recruitment process. Secondly, training will need to be provided for officers with personnel responsibilities, to ensure that all staff regardless of racial and ethnic group are treated equally with regards to postings and career development, and that grievance and discipline procedures relating to discrimination operate effectively. Thirdly, all staff (and especially supervisors) will need training to ensure that multi-ethnic staffing is accepted throughout the organisation and functions effectively, without any forms of exclusionary pressure (e.g. jokes and harassment) on members of minority groups.

- *Access training*

Finally, it may be appropriate to provide special "access" training for candidates from migrant or minority ethnic backgrounds, as part of "positive action" programmes designed to increase entry into the police service from such groups. These courses are intended to equip potential recruits from minority or migrant backgrounds with linguistic, educational and other skills necessary for them to compete for entry on an equal basis with other candidates, or to assist them to attain fixed entry standards where these are set. Access training schemes have been introduced in the Netherlands (see sections I.8 and I.13 below), and by the West Midlands Police in the UK (see Commission for Racial Equality 1991).

Aims and objectives

Before beginning to design any training programmes for police officers on matters concerning migrants and ethnic relations, it is essential to make clear the aims and objectives of such training. In the present document it is only possible to consider the aims and objectives of such training at the most general level.

(a)   Overall aim

The Meeting of Experts on police training on matters concerning migrants and ethnic relations agreed in its "Conclusions" that the overall aim of training in this field should be expressed positively and in terms of general principles of good professional practice. The aim as formulated identified the relevant principles as "equality", "fairness" and "individual need", principles that should be applied in treatment of all members of the public regardless of social group:

> "To promote in the police service the equal and fair treatment of all members of the public according to their individual needs."

As the Meeting of Experts continued:

> "This means combating all forms of discrimination - not only those directed against immigrant and ethnic groups. It is also necessary to respond adequately to the diversity of the population, including its cultural diversity."

-      *Commentary on overall aim*

This formulation, which must be commended to all police training organisations in Europe, has three particular strengths which should be retained even if a different wording were to be adopted:

(a)　　the aim is defined in positive terms (i.e. to promote fairness and equality), but the obstacle (i.e. discrimination) is also identified within this framework;

(b)　　the aim is defined in general terms (i.e. to promote equality, and combat discrimination, generally), but the specific concerns (i.e. migrants and ethnic relations) are also identified within this framework;

(c)　　in so far as the aim is specific to matters of migrants and ethnic relations, it identifies the need to respond positively to cultural diversity, as well as negatively to ethnic, racial or xenophobic discrimination.

(b)　Objectives

The Meeting of Experts identified six specific objectives that need to be attained within police training if this overall aim is to be achieved. These were as follows:

1.　　To advance the knowledge and understanding of the police officer in the field of human relations;

2.　　To develop better communication skills, especially in the multicultural context;

3.　　To enhance the capacity of the police to provide a high quality of service to the public;

4.　　To respect all individuals, irrespective of their origin;

5.　　To strengthen the confidence of the police in fulfilling their functions in a multicultural society;

6.　　To improve police officers' knowledge of the law and regulations relevant to immigrants and racial discrimination.

- *Application to all training programmes*

These objectives should be included as part of the overall framework of objectives for police training in every European country. They should be included among the broad objectives for both initial and in-service training, so that they may be achieved for all police officers at all levels. It will be especially important for them to be addressed at the initial stage of training, so that a solid foundation is laid at the outset of an officer's career. It is also important to include them in in- service training at all subsequent stages of an officer's career, both as part of "professional development" training and in preparation for specialist and managerial roles.

- *General and specific objectives*

Several of the objectives, in accordance with the overall aim of training set out above, are formulated in general terms rather than in terms specific to matters concerning migrants and ethnic relations. This emphasises that dealing effectively with matters concerning migrants and ethnic relations is in large part a question of good policing practice generally: of good human relations, of good communication skills, of high quality service provision, and of respect for all individuals regardless of origin. Where such general objectives are already addressed, it is important to ensure that migrant/ethnic-specific objectives are specified within them.

Correspondingly, where migrant/ethnic specific objectives are set, it is important that they are addressed in the context of training designed to achieve the basic skills and understanding required by effective policing in general.

Training designed to address matters concerning migrants and ethnic relations will not be effective unless a sound foundation has already been laid. This has been very clearly recognised, for example, in the new initial training programme devised for the Norwegian police (see section I.9 below). This programme has been designed to provide a very thorough social science basis for the training of police officers to serve the public in a diverse and changing world.

- *Rank/role-specific objectives*

Within each country, and for training courses for particular ranks and roles, more specific objectives will need to prepared, based on those set out above. It is not possible in a general document of this kind to draw up rank- or role-specific objectives in the necessary detail, and in any event important national differences in police organisation and function would have to be taken into account. It is important, however, that the rank-specific objectives should form a developmental sequence, with each building on the attainments of the rank below. An example of a set of rank/role-specific objectives forming a developmental sequence is provided in the training strategy formulated by the British Police Training Council in 1983, currently being updated by the Home Office Specialist Support Unit (see section I.13 below and Police Training Council 1983). Although this scheme has been designed to suit the British context, it could readily be adapted for use elsewhere.

Content of training

The Meeting of Experts identified two main areas which should be covered by the content of training:

    (a)   knowledge and understanding;
    (b)   behaviour.

Of these two, behaviour was seen as crucial, since it is behaviour that constitutes police service to the public, and not simply the knowledge or understanding that lies behind it. Both these areas are considered in detail below. The question of addressing a third content area, that of attitudes, is also considered.

(a)   Knowledge and Understanding

The experts stressed that the specific knowledge and understanding of matters concerning migrants and ethnic relations should at all times be founded in general social science knowledge and in professional ethics based on human rights. Police training currently varies between different European countries in the extent to which it is based in the social sciences and in human rights, and this variation accounts for some very different approaches taken in different countries to training on migrant and ethnic issues. These different approaches are documented in the paper summarising the results of the Europe-wide survey of police training practice in this field (see section II below). An example of a training strongly founded in the social sciences would be the recruit training being introduced in Norway, while in neighbouring Sweden may be found an example of a special programme dealing with migrant and ethnic issues which is closely linked to training in human rights (see sections I.9 and I.10 below).

-   *Core curriculum components*

The experts attending the Meeting identified the following list of topics as needing to be covered under the heading of "knowledge and understanding". This list should be regarded as components of a "core curriculum" based on the objectives set out above, a curriculum which in an appropriate manner should be incorporated into the overall training curriculum for all police officers in every European country. Further comment on some of the topics will be made below.

(a)   social, historical, legal and cultural aspects of migration and the situation of populations of immigrant origin;

(b)   cultural pluralism in society, and the need for respect for different value systems;

(c)   awareness of the often unstated assumptions of the dominant culture and of ethnocentrism;

(d)   the role of the police in society;

(e)   the concepts of prejudice and discrimination, including both personal and institutional discrimination;

(f)   analysis of racism and xenophobia, including their manifestation in the form of violence and harassment;

(g)   the variety of minority responses to dominance.

- *Ethnocentrism and Cultural Pluralism*

To achieve the objectives set for police training in this field, it will be necessary (but not sufficient) to provide officers with information on the different aspects of migration and the situation of immigrant groups. It is also essential to ensure that officers recognise that Europe has now become a culturally plural society, and are able to identify the implications for themselves as police officers. Whatever their personal views on this matter, as professionals it is their role to provide a public service to a culturally diverse community, and this requires respect for the diverse value systems.

Hitherto it has been possible for police professionals and their organisations to function as if they operated in a mono-ethnic society. If they are to provide a fair and equal service to all sections of the multi-cultural society, it will be of crucial importance for them to become aware of how ethnocentric assumptions of the dominant culture may shape police thinking and practice - with often unintended discriminatory effects. All police officers working in a multi-cultural context should be capable of recognising ethnocentrism as a normal tendency, yet also one that needs to be countered. An example of how this issue may be addressed in training is provided by the course taught at the Danish Police College (see section I.2 below). Great importance is also attached to the need to address ethnocentrism in the training programmes in Britain and the Netherlands.

- *Prejudice and Discrimination*

In a modern democratic society, all public service professionals need to have a sound understanding of the nature of prejudice and discrimination, and an appreciation of how these are capable of obstructing the overall aim of delivering a fair and equal service to all members of the public according to individual need. Police officers need a sound understanding of prejudice and discrimination generally, as well as of the causes and manifestations that relate to migrant and ethnic groups in particular. Among the specific topics that need to be addressed in police training under this heading are:

(a)   how values, attitudes and prejudices are formed in the process of socialisation;

(b)   the nature and function of stereotypes, and how they obstruct fair and equal treatment of members of the public as individuals;

(c)   the reasons why police officers may come under pressure to develop prejudices, stereotypes and cynicism generally, especially due to their prevalence in police culture and to the nature and organisational context of police work;

(d)   the distinction between personal discrimination, which is the acting out of individual prejudices; and institutional discrimination, which is a result of the "normal" policies and practices of an organisation that may be discriminatory in effect, often without awareness or intent on the part of staff as individuals.

- *Racism and Xenophobia*

Prejudice and discrimination against migrants and minority ethnic groups is predominantly expressed in the form of racism and xenophobia. Police training programmes in every European country should include a component ensuring that all police officers have a sound understanding of the nature of racism and xenophobia, together with an appreciation of the threat they pose to democracy and human rights, and to the fabric of European society generally. In particular, the manifestations of racism and xenophobia in the form of violence and harassment should receive special attention. This is because of their increasing prevalence in Europe, and their damaging effects not only for the victims, but on the sense of security and well-being of visible minority communities everywhere - and thus on community relations in general. The special responsibility of the police in tackling this problem should be stressed. General documentation and guidance on this subject is available in a report prepared for the Council of Europe (Oakley 1992; see also European Parliament 1990), while an example of detailed practical guidance for the police is contained in a British Government report on the problem in the UK (Home Office 1989).

-     *Minority Responses to Dominance*

Lastly, among topics of major importance in the field of knowledge and understanding, special attention should be given to ensuring that all police officers have a sound understanding of the responses of members of minority groups to perceived discrimination and to dominance generally. Police officers need to understand the diversity of such responses, and the dynamics of majority-minority relations, so that they are able to intervene effectively so as to maintain both order and justice, and promote good community relations generally. The understanding required is, once again, a general understanding of this phenomenon - an understanding of how any persons may respond when they perceive themselves to be under threat or subject to dominance. Police officers too will have such experiences in certain situations, although for members of minorities it will be the police who are perceived to be in the dominant position. However, it is important that police officers can apply their general understanding of this phenomenon to situations involving migrants and visible minorities. Special attention should be given to two areas:

(a)   minority responses to racial violence and harassment, where it has not been uncommon for victims to get arrested on account of their reactions rather than the perpetrators; and

(b)   interventions by police (e.g. street stops), which - however skilful, sensitive and non-discriminatory - may be responded to by minority persons in the light of perceptions and expectations rooted in a history of negative experiences of police and other agencies shared within that minority group.

-      *The experience of women*

In considering all of the above areas of content and understanding, car should be taken to ensure that the distinct experiences of women within migrant and minority ethnic communities are not overlooked. Women members of such communities may frequently experience "double" disadvantage and discrimination, due to gender as well as to racial or ethnic origin. In addition, in many minority ethnic communities, traditional cultural values relating to women differ from those of Western European cultures, sometimes giving rise to conflicts and dilemmas in which police may become involved. Training should therefore ensure that police officers have both awareness and understanding of the circumstances of women in such communities, so that they can be sensitive and responsive to women's needs as well as those of men. The European Network of Policewomen, as well as women's organisations within Member States, may be able to provide further guidance in this area.

(b)   Behaviour

With regard to the behavioural content of training, the Experts again stressed that the particular skills and abilities required in dealing with matters concerning migrants and ethnic relations were for the most part the same broad skills and abilities required for good policing practice generally. However, some of these capabilities might be severely tested in situations where officers are unfamiliar with particular ethnic groups and their cultural background, and where there may be strong feelings around issues of racism and discrimination.

- *Core curriculum components*

The Meeting of Experts listed the following set of topics as needing to be covered under the heading of "behaviour". As before, this list should be regarded as components of a "core curriculum", which should be incorporated in an appropriate manner into the overall training curriculum for all police officers in every European country. Further comment on some of the topics is made in subsequent paragraphs:

(a)   how to communicate effectively and avoid misunderstandings in intercultural situations;

(b)   management of violence and conflict;

(c)   how to cope with stress and fear on the part of the police officer;

(d)   the unacceptability of discriminatory behaviour; and the skills and confidence needed to challenge such behaviour, especially when it is encountered among colleagues;

(e)   the positive professional standards of conduct required of officers in multi-cultural and multi-racial situations.

- *Cross-cultural communication*

Special attention should be paid to the need to equip officers with skills of effective communication in inter-cultural situations. First of all, officers should be able to identify situations where interpreters are required, as well as recognising the limitations of third-party interpretation. Secondly, officers should recognise that those who are not fluent in a language may often not use words in the same way as native speakers, or may not understand a native speaker in the way that person assumes. Thirdly, officers should take great care in the way they "read" (often unconsciously) the "body language" of persons of migrant or minority ethnic origin, since this may not have the same meaning as in the dominant culture (e.g. eye contact, and various body movements). Officers should also take care as to how they comport themselves in inter-cultural situations, so that they do not convey unintended messages (e.g. inducing fear or defensiveness) that may obstruct their work. Particular sensitivity and skill is therefore required of officers if they are to avoid misunderstandings and communicate effectively in inter-cultural situations. This subject has already begun to be addressed in several countries, and video materials are used in Britain and the Netherlands.

- *Tackling discrimination*

Tackling discrimination is a second area of behaviour in which special skills and abilities are required, or at least in which general skills must be applied effectively. The police role involves not only tackling discrimination in the community where it constitutes an offence; it also requires ensuring that police behaviour itself is not discriminatory. When discriminatory behaviour takes place, or prejudices are openly expressed, it may be difficult for a fellow-officer to respond, especially among peers or when the person is a more senior officer. Yet it must be the professional responsibility of *all* officers to address this issue. It should certainly not be left to officers of migrant or minority origin to deal with the problem (nor to women alone to deal with sexism). Equipping officers with the skills and confidence to deal with discrimination *within* as well as outside the organisation is an essential topic for inclusion within police training. Otherwise stereotyping and forms of inappropriate behaviour will persist unchallenged, to the detriment of professional standards, staffing, quality of service, and public trust generally.

(c)   Attitudes

The question of whether attitudes on matters concerning migrants and ethnic relations should form part of the content of police training gave rise to considerable debate in the Meeting of Experts. This reflects a wider debate on how professional training in general should address attitudes, and indeed on whether it is possible to change attitudes through training.

-   *The need to address attitudes*

The general view of the meeting was that the attitudes of police officers are of great importance in determining their behaviour. It was noted that many shortcomings in police behaviour in this area clearly arose from the existence of prejudice and stereotyping, and from lack of respect for other cultures and ethnic groups. It was also noted, e.g. from early British experience of police training on these issues (see Oakley 1990; also Luthra and Oakley 1991), that simply providing information about other cultures or migrant groups did not of itself create respect, let alone guarantee appropriate behaviour. It was concluded therefore that it was not sufficient to address skills and knowledge alone in training, but that attitudes too need to be addressed in some way.

-   *Approach attitudes through professionalism*

The experts were strongly of the opinion, however, that to tackle attitudes directly and in a judgemental way in training would be ineffective. It was felt that this would be particularly dangerous with experienced officers, whose reaction might be the opposite to that intended. A similar conclusion may be drawn from an experiment with "Racism Awareness Training" courses conducted for British police officers in the early 1980s (see Southgate 1984). Rather, the approach to be taken should be one of enhancing professionalism generally among police officers, and defining clearly the ethics and standards required. Respect for others, and the provision of fair and equal treatment to all should be central components of such professionalism, with which all officers would be expected to comply. Initial training would seek to establish a foundation of such attitudes, while in-service training would seek to maintain them and develop their application in police work. Attitudes on matters concerning migrants and ethnic relations would be addressed strictly within this positive and professionally-oriented framework.

- *The importance of self-awareness*

The danger remains that personal attitudes on migrant and ethnic issues might still obstruct this positive, professional approach. Training should not be expected to resolve serious attitude problems, such as those arising from the presence of officers with firmly racist, anti-semitic, or xenophobic views. Nor should it be regarded as remedial treatment for officers who deliberately discriminate against or harass persons of migrant or minority ethnic origin. These are matters for selection and discipline. Instead, the role of training with regard to personal attitudes should not primarily be to change them, but to enable officers to become *aware* of their own (often unconscious) feelings and opinions on racial and ethnic issues. By this means, i.e. through reflection, they can take account of their own attitudes and through personal reflection question these where appropriate, and try to ensure that personal attitudes do not obstruct the professionalism with which they seek to carry out their policing role.

- *Conclusion*

The conclusion of the Experts, therefore, was that in the short-term (and especially with experienced officers), training should be focused primarily on behavioural skills and the standards of behaviour expected of officers by the organisation, without directly challenging attitudes. Insofar as attitudes are to be addressed, this should be primarily (and especially in initial training) through emphasis on the need for professionalism generally, which should be applied in multi-racial and multi-cultural contexts no less than elsewhere. Any direct focus on personal attitudes on migrant and ethnic issues should not attempt to judge or directly change such views, but rather assist officers to become aware of them and to reflect on their implications.

In the long run, experience (backed by behaviourist theory) suggests that it will be through the positive learning opportunities created by a behaviour-oriented approach that more positive personal attitudes among police officers on racial and ethnic issues will be generated. That is to say, it was the view of the Experts that attitude change should be largely expected to *follow* behaviour change rather than to precede it. However, it is important that this should not be left to chance, but that there should be a definite *educational* strategy within police continuation training to promote and achieve this goal.

Methods

The Meeting of Experts stressed that the above content, viewed as a "core curriculum", should be incorporated into national police training programmes in all European countries, and delivered to all officers in a manner appropriate to their role. The Experts considered that the training should be mandatory for all officers, and its purpose presented as to enhance professionalism in the context of a changing and increasingly pluralistic society. A variety of different training methods should be employed, from which particular methods should be selected according to their appropriateness to the topic and the rank and role of the participants.

- *Three levels of training*

Three broad levels of officer responsibility for service delivery were distinguished within the organisation, for each of which a distinctive approach to training should be undertaken. These were (a) front-line officers, for whom the training should be provided at the stage at which they are recruited; (b) officers with supervisory and middle-management responsibility; and (c) senior officers with executive responsibility.

Recruits: training should provide for the basic knowledge and skills set out under "Content" above, as a basic professional foundation for all police officers carrying out a public service role in a multi-cultural and multi-racial society.

Middle managers: training should ensure possession of the basic knowledge and skills (using catch-up provision if necessary), and add to this the further understanding and abilities required by supervisors and managers to enable them to ensure that all officers under their personal command deliver a fair and equal service to migrants and minorities along with all other sections of the public.

Senior Officers: training should ensure the ability to address matters concerning migrants and ethnic relations at a policy and strategic level for the organisation as a whole, and to set and implement corporate standards in dealing with such issues.

- *Senior Officer Responsibility*

Senior officers should not only receive training in this area (and be seen to do so), but should actively sponsor and support such training throughout the organisation. This will include personal oversight of the design and execution of training programmes and willingness to open and participate in special courses arranged from time to time on these subjects. Any special training programme in this field should proceed from the top of the organisation downwards. Senior officers should also ensure than police unions have been consulted: the unions should be invited to contribute and give the programme their full support.

- *Classroom methods*

Classroom methods of training should include a wide variety of learning methods, and should not be restricted to specialist lectures or talks, as has often been the case with training on this subject in the past. The full range of training methods nowadays in use in police training establishments should be applied in this area, including role-plays, structured exercises, group discussions, and video presentations. In general, the merits and shortcomings of these various methods will be well-known to those responsible for training, but some specific comments relating to their application to training on racial and ethnic issues are given below. Whatever methods are used, it is extremely important that adequate *time* (and where possible flexibility of arrangements) is allowed for addressing these issues, since they tend to be sensitive and controversial, and strong feelings may require skilled and patient processing within the training group.

- *Role-plays*

The use of role-plays as a vehicle for experiential learning is increasingly recognised in police training, but successful use requires a high degree of skill and sensitivity on the part of the trainer. This is especially so when dealing with racial and ethnic issues, where powerful emotions may be aroused. Special care must be taken in assigning officers (whether black or white) to racial roles, or where background knowledge (e.g. cultural or religious) is required which they do not possess. It may be appropriate to engage students or actors to play migrant or visible minority roles, either in company with police officers, or as a separate dramatic presentation to the course participants. Both these methods have been used in the Netherlands and Britain. The Metropolitan Police in London invite members of community groups to participate in recruit training, and (under trainer supervision) to devise and act in role-plays based on their personal experience.

- *Video*

Video is a valuable resource in police training on matters concerning migrants and ethnic relations - for imparting information, for bringing experience into the classroom under controlled conditions, and for triggering debate on controversial issues. Obtaining suitable video materials to meet precise training needs, however, is often difficult. Much of the video material used in police training was not devised for this purpose, and while some has proved extremely successful, there are frequently problems of relevance and credibility. (There may also be problems of obtaining permission to use documentary and film material for police training purposes.) Producing videos specifically for police training purposes can be a time-consuming and costly exercise, and police audiences are never more critical than when the subject of the video is the police organisation itself. Nonetheless, videos specially designed for use in police training on issues such as the background of immigrant groups, cross-cultural communication, and racially motivated attacks have been produced in different countries (including France, the Netherlands and Britain).

-   *Written materials*

Written materials play an important part in training on matters concerning migrants and ethnic relations. Written materials are mainly used to achieve knowledge objectives: knowledge of such matters as the history of migration, relevant policy and legislation, key concepts such as prejudice and discrimination, and the cultures and experiences of migrants and minority groups. In France, reports of national seminars on these subjects as they affect policing present in-depth and expert analyses of the problems. In Berlin, a booklet presenting factual information about foreigners in Berlin is used to inform police officers on the subject during training (see sections I.4 and I.5 below). In Britain, West Yorkshire police, in conjunction with local community groups, have produced a similar booklet for use in training and by police officers generally.

However, it is important that information provision alone should not be regarded as sufficient. Other training activities, such as exercises and personal contact with members of such communities, should be used as well to enhance empathy and understanding, and to demonstrate the relevance and usefulness of the knowledge in everyday police work. For example, in Britain the West Midlands Police have produced an extended "case-study" on racial harassment, which is capable of being used in classroom activities in a variety of ways. The Recruit

Training School of London's Metropolitan Police have produced a comprehensive "handbook" entitled *Fair Treatment for All*, which includes not only factual information but also exercises of various kinds. The handbook is designed to be a resource to support a series of "focus sessions" on issues concerning minority communities and equal opportunities which form part of the wider recruit training curriculum.

- *Training design: some general principles*

The Meeting of Experts formulated some guiding principles which should be followed so far as possible in designing training programmes addressing matters concerning migrants and ethnic relations. These may be summarised as follows:

(a)   the professional experience of trainees should be respected and used a resource for learning, as well as being a source for identifying training needs;

(b)   localised training provision in this field should be developed, so as to ensure that content is diversified to meet local needs, and that the training is closely integrated with the workplace;

(c)   multi-agency training should be developed in order to enhance mutual understanding and cooperation between public-service professionals;

(d)   there should be direct community involvement especially of migrant and minority ethnic groups in police training, and in particular for the purpose of creating opportunities for learning through personal contact with members of such groups;

(e)   persons (both women and men) of migrant or minority ethnic origin should be included among the training instructors, undertaking training in ethnically and gender-mixed teams;

(f)   specialist training should be provided for all training staff to enable them to deliver training on racial and ethnic issues effectively.

- *Community involvement in police training*

Particular importance should be attached to the development of community involvement in police training. Such involvement may be arranged in a variety of ways. Talks by community representatives, meetings with groups of young people, visits to community centres and religious institutions, placements in local agencies or families - these are some of many possibilities. Special attention should be paid to securing the participation of women as well as men in these arrangements, especially in ethnic communities where women traditionally have been less involved in affairs outside the home. Care and sensitivity need to be used in arranging and carrying out initiatives of this kind, and ensuring that they produce positive learning and are felt to have been beneficial by both sides. Meetings and visits should be carefully planned, managed and debriefed. They should not be treated casually or allowed to progress in an uncontrolled way. Community involvement should be regarded as a two-way process, with a partnership approach and with involvement in the design as well as the delivery of training. In Britain, the Home Office-funded Specialist Support Unit has developed a number of initiatives in this field, included weekend residential placements with visible minority families (see section I.13 below). London's Metropolitan Police have developed a "Reciprocal Training Scheme" within their recruit training programme, and have established a special "Community Involvement Unit" to manage this and other initiatives.

- *Training for trainers*

The provision of specialist training for all training staff is also of particular importance in developing practice in this area of police training. Experience in Britain has shown that even though training materials are available and topics included in the curriculum, the delivery of training on racial and ethnic issues will not be effective unless the trainers themselves are knowledgeable, skilled and confident in dealing with such issues. In the Netherlands, specialist training for trainers has been provided by the independent Anne Frank Centre under government funding. In Britain, the Home Office-funded Specialist Support Unit provides intensive six-week residential courses on "community and race relations" for selected trainers from police training schools, whose role is also to act as training development agents in their own training establishments (see sections I.8 and I.13 below).

-      *Recruitment and Selection*

Special provision will need to be made for the training of persons responsible for recruitment and selection. All police organisations should seek to ensure equal opportunity for persons of migrant or minority ethnic origin in access to employment in the police, and should aim that the ethnic composition of police staff should broadly reflect the ethnic composition of the community. Experience in Britain and the Netherlands has shown that this will not come about either of its own accord, or merely through campaigns to encourage applications from minority communities. Many institutional barriers exist which place minority persons at a disadvantage, and there must be identified and removed. These barriers include the following: language; unfamiliarity with the dominant culture; nationality/citizenship requirements; ethnic bias in selection tests (normed on the dominant culture); negative experience of policing; negative attitudes towards minorities within the police culture; lack of confidence in career prospects for minority officers; and fear of discriminatory posting (e.g. to minority communities). Officers responsible for recruitment and selection need training to ensure that they can use relevant methodology (e.g. interviews, written and physical examinations, assessment centres) in a manner that is without ethnic bias. Such training has been carried out extensively in both the Netherlands and Britain (e.g. work of the Anne Frank Centre, Amsterdam; Metropolitan Police, London) (see section I.8 below).

Implementation

Many proposals for the development of police training on matters concerning migrants and ethnic relations have been set out above. It is recommended that these proposals should be adopted in the training of police officers throughout Europe. However, such proposals will have no value unless they are effectively implemented.

- *Role of Senior Police management*

It has already been stressed earlier in this document that the responsibility for the implementation of these proposals lies with senior police management, and that these proposals should receive their active support. In each country it will be necessary for senior management: (a) to acknowledge the general need for matters concerning migrants and ethnic relations to be addressed in training; (b) to identify the specific form taken by these needs in the particular case; and (c) to formulate an appropriate response at policy level. This process may require research to be undertaken, and advice should be sought from experts with prior experience of work in this field.

- *Migrant/Minority involvement at policy level*

The process should also involve consultation with appropriate representatives of migrant and minority ethnic communities, using existing institutional structures where available - or creating new mechanisms for the purpose if required. Such consultation might include a series of consultative seminars aimed at identifying needs and reviewing proposed responses respectively. In Britain, the national Commission for Racial Equality has direct involvement in policy development on this aspect of police training. In several other countries too, national bodies representing the interests of migrant and minority ethnic groups have been involved in this process. These include Belgium (Commissariat Royal à la Politique des Immigrés); France (Commission Nationale Consultative des Droits de l'Homme); Sweden

(Ombudsman Against Discrimination); and in Germany the cities of Berlin (Ombudsman for Foreigners) and Frankfurt (Office for Multi-cultural Affairs) (see section I.1 and I.6 below).

- *The need for strategy*

The implementation of these proposals should not consist of a collection of uncoordinated initiatives, but should take the form of a clear overall strategy for the development of this aspect of police training. The strategy should set out clear goals and means of achieving them. At the practical level, it should be translated into specific plans for the introduction and coordination of the various activities. The plans should include clear time-scales for the achievement of tasks, and allocations of responsibilities to officers or sections of the training organisation. It will be necessary to assign overall responsibility for implementation to a particular officer, who may require assistance in the form of a dedicated and appropriately staffed "support unit".

- *Role of governmental authorities*

Support for the development of such training activities will be required not only from senior police management, but also from higher authorities at governmental level. This is likely to be necessary for the requisite level of resources to be made available for programmes of this kind. Resources available within routine budgets will probably not be adequate for the purpose. The willingness to release additional resources will be a demonstration of the commitment of the authorities to support such programmes; if they have been specially funded, the authorities will have an interest in ensuring that their implementation has been effective. In the Netherlands, government and senior police management work together to promote training development in this field: this is done within the framework of a national policy that has been approved by the Dutch Parliament, and the Dutch Home Office has been able to deploy funding to ensure that appropriate initiatives are taken forward in accordance with the overall plan. The British Home

Office directly funds an independent "Specialist Support Unit" which assists police forces throughout Britain to develop this aspect of police training. The new training initiatives currently being introduced in Norway also have the authority and support of the Norwegian Parliament. (See sections I.7; I.8; I.9; I.12 and I.13 below)

- *Evaluation and review*

The progress of the implementation of police training strategy in this field should not be left to evolve of its own accord, but should be subject to regular monitoring and review. Internal and external evaluation of training courses should be conducted regularly and systematically. The results of this evaluation should be fed back at management level into policy and strategy review. In the light of the degree of effectiveness shown, it may prove necessary to adjust the objectives, the content and the methods of training. Ways should be found to involve representatives of migrant and minority ethnic communities in this monitoring and review process.

- *The importance of a proactive response*

At the present time there is a tendency for many initiatives to remain at an experimental stage. Due to the urgency of developing training for police officers on matters concerning migrants and ethnic relations, it is important that the authorities move rapidly to establish such initiatives on a more permanent basis within mainstream police training, so that all police officers may benefit from them rather than a selected few. Police organisations should not wait for the pressure of events (e.g. public disorders with a racial or xenophobic aspect) to force them into taking action in this field: it is essential to act *before* such incidents may occur, so as to ensure that police are ready to deal with such situations and are equipped to perform their role in all sections of Europe's ethnically diverse communities.

The importance of a proactive response is highlighted by the British experience of inner-city rioting in 1981. The sudden escalation of racial and xenophobic violence across Europe during the early 1990s further emphasises the same point. In this context it was alarming to find from the questionnaire survey that relatively little specific attention appeared to be being given to the subject of racism and xenophobia in police training in Europe. Given currents trends in racial and xenophobic violence, and the crucial importance of the police role in tackling the problem, this is a subject which should be integrated proactively and indeed urgently in all mainstream police training throughout Europe.

-    *The need for European cooperation*

Nonetheless, it should be recognised that ill-conceived initiatives introduced with undue haste are unlikely to prove effective and may indeed be counter-productive in their effect. One way to be able to move quickly without making such errors is to learn from others either within the country or in other European states. Whilst an initiative developed in one country will probably not be appropriate for another country in precisely its original design, it may well be appropriate in an adapted form.

Cross-national cooperation is essential if each state (or individual police organisation) is to avoid delayed response while each "reinvents the wheel". At policy level such cooperation should be undertaken by governments and senior police management, using existing structures of governmental and police cooperation. At practitioner level, Europe-wide networks have already begun to be established at a personal level, and these should be formalised and supported (including financially) by senior police management. The Council of Europe, with its pan-European constituency, its responsibilities relating to education and human rights, and its capacity to bring together all parties concerned with these issues, should continue to promote and give support to development work in this field, which is of great importance for the future of Europe's multi-ethnic society.

Robin Oakley
Consultant

References

Commission Nationale Consultative des Droits de l'Homme, *1991: La Lutte contre le Racisme et la Xenophobie*, La Documentation Française, Paris 1992

Commission for Racial Equality, *Policing and Racial Equality*, CRE, London 1993

Commission for Racial Equality, *Police Access Training: A Case-Study of Positive Action and Ethnic Minority Recruitment to the West Midlands Police Force*, CRE, London 1992

Council of Europe, *Community and Ethnic Relations in Europe: Final Report of the Community Relations Project of the Council of Europe*, Council of Europe, Strasbourg 1991

European Parliament, *Committee of Enquiry into Racism and Xenophobia: Report on the Findings of the Committee of Enquiry*, European Parliament, Luxembourg 1990

Home Office, *Racial Attacks and Harassment: Guidance for the Statutory Agencies*, London, Home Office 1989

Leinen M, *Black Police, White Society*, New York University Press, 1984

Luthra M & Oakley R, *Combatting Racism through Training: a Review of Approaches to Race Training in Organisations*, University of Warwick 1991

Oakley R, "Police Training on Ethnic Relations in Britain", *Police Studies: the International Review of Police Development*, Vol.13, No.2 (Summer 1990)

Oakley R, *Policing and Race Equality in the Netherlands: Positive Action Initiatives in Recruitment and Training*, Police Foundation, London 1990

Oakley R, "Learning from the Community: Facilitated Police-Community Workshops at the Local Level", in Marshall T (editor), *Community Disorders and Policing*, Whiting and Birch, London 1992

Oakley R, *Racial Violence and Harassment in Europe*, Council of Europe 1992

Police Training Council, *Community and Race Relations Training for the Police*, Home Office, London 1983

Southgate P, *Racism Awareness Training for the Police*, Home Office, London 1984

1. Royal Commission
for Immigrant Policy,
Brussels, Belgium

Information project for members of the
Belgian Administration, Police and Gendarmerie

"BUILDING AWARENESS OF IMMIGRANT ISSUES"

In March 1989 the Belgian Government appointed a Royal Commissioner for Immigrant Policy for a term of four years. The Royal Commission received instructions to analyze the situation and suggest measures for the integration of immigrants into Belgian society, with special attention to employment, housing and education.

The government has approved the integration concept which has four main aspects:

- full applicability to migrants of Belgian law, amendable only by normal parliamentary procedure; public order is to be strictly observed;

- consistent promotion of the fullest possible integration, in accordance with the basic social principles underlying the host country's culture and pertaining to "modernism", "emancipation" and "resolute pluralism" as understood by a modern Western state;

- unequivocal respect for cultural diversity as a source of mutual enrichment in other relevant areas;

- the three aspects mentioned above entail more systematic involvement of minorities in the activities and objectives of the public authorities.

In order to improve contact between nationals and immigrants, a proposal was made for "specific action aimed at the staff of administrative departments and at persons with an education and training function".

Objective

Living in a multi-ethnic society alongside people with different cultures, religions and traditions is not straightforward. Information and training on the cultural background of immigrants can in some cases help determine a "positive" approach to certain situations perceived as "problematic". Moreover, it is very important that immigrants and Belgian officials develop positive images of one another.

The Royal Commission intends the information programme on "*Building awareness of immigrant issues*" for members of the police, the gendarmerie and the administration because we are conscious that these groups of officials have a lot to do with immigrants. The programme aims to make the concept of "integration" applicable on the ground.

Recapitulation

An enquiry from the Royal Commission indicated that 25 municipalities in Flanders were interested in the information programme "*Building awareness of immigrant issues*". These authorities were able to fund the project with assistance from either the Flemish Fund for the Integration of the Disadvantaged or the Local Government Fund.

A French language version of the programme was concurrently devised in order to offer a similar facility to the municipalities of Brussels and Wallonia.

The Ministry of the Interior took an interest in the project and released the funds needed to run a corresponding project for police officers.

It was initially carried out in four Flemish municipalities with a high immigrant population (Antwerp, Mechlin, Mol and Louvain). It had a successful outcome which, following the riots by young immigrants in Brussels in May 1991, prompted a decision to broaden the scope of action to cover the police forces of 10 Brussels municipalities. After the Brussels incidents, the gendarmerie also realised the need for such information programmes.

So far approximately 1000 officials, policemen and gendarmes from some 20 towns and municipalities have taken part in the project since its commencement in January 1990.

As the duration of the programme is only 25 hours, it is presented to candidates as an information rather than a training offer. This is why the scheme is regarded more as an "introduction to immigrant issues".

The aim is to provide a broader view of the issues. A discussion on certain problem situations may bring about some changes in attitudes.

Content

The programme consists of three principal modules:

- **Basic information** (3 x 3 h 30)

  History and development of immigration, current situation, demography, cultural and religious origins, young immigrants, etc.

- **Practical information** (2 x 3 h 30):

  Discussions on practical experience, breakdown of communication, conflict situations, etc.

- **A day for contact in the field** (7 h 30):

    Encounter between the participants and the local immigrant population in a community setting (youth centre, mosque, women's club, etc).

Participants must be able to discuss their grievances with the instructors. They are assured that unpleasant experiences and ill-feeling towards immigrants must be discussed even if the subject has emotional implications, provided that the parties are prepared to listen to each other and the discussion is constructive.

The Royal Commission co-operates with the police and gendarmerie training colleges by offering single sessions on immigration as this topic is not yet covered in the training syllabus.

Participants

The lectures are theoretically intended for persons actively dealing with immigrants in their work, including patrolmen, neighbourhood constables and counter staff.

Participation must be voluntary; this is a most important factor. The topic of immigration tends to arouse strong emotions which are frequently divergent. Before embarking on the information programme, potential participants are asked to fill in a form stating their expectations which is used to assess their interest. Prospective participants sometimes explicitly refuse to take part, a reason commonly put forward being that they "feel humiliated by this proposal".

Convinced or persistent opponents of immigrants are not the target group of the information programme, whose optimum effect is attainable by dialogue alone. A minimum degree of motivation is therefore required. This requirement must not be underestimated: the effort demanded is a substantial one for many participants as the programme covers a full week and the subjects addressed are not straightforward.

Not only must participants be persuaded that it is worthwhile to take part; in addition the local authorities and the heads of the respective departments must appreciate the need for the programme and give it full support.

A briefing is held to give potential candidates an overview of the information programme in the presence of the instructors and the local leaders. This phase is decisive in facilitating enrolment. Moral support but above all direct information are vitally important at the time of enrolment.

Instructors

The Royal Commission has only three instructors to run the information programme. Consequently, we enlist the aid of two training institutions: *Trasporti Interculturali* (Dutch speaking) and *Synergie* (French speaking) who provide us with instructors on a freelance co-operation basis.

The persons concerned have the necessary qualifications to take charge of such programmes (criminologists, sociologists, social workers) and are experienced with regard to migration issues and training.

Each new assistant receives prior training and is supported during the initial assignments by the Royal Commission. At present we have about a dozen instructors, half of foreign origin.

"Key witnesses"

In each municipality, we call upon a "*key witness*", a person - preferably of foreign origin - who attends the information programme in order to illustrate the local situation. This is also the person who makes contact with the immigrant associations to be visited. This "*key witness*" may later become the person to be contacted by the police when, for instance, friction occurs between Belgians and immigrants or between police officers and young immigrants.

Concise appraisal

The following reaction by police officers is often recorded: why is it they who must adjust to immigrants by undergoing the information programme on immigrants. This reaction is understandable; many officers currently serving in large cities have little or no time to temper their action with a social approach.

The groups regarded as "identifiable suspects" form the public whom police officers most readily encounter in their daily duties. These groups are familiar: young people who attract attention by their demeanour or appearance, immigrants who are "different" in any case, refugees who to all appearances are "illegals", etc. The police often have difficulties with these groups. Their function requires them to ensure the safety of the public.

Police officers are often confronted with those individuals who infringe the prescribed rules and even the laws of Belgium. "Law-abiding" is an expression which can have a subjective connotation. Subjectiveness can even predominate in the way the police officer does his job and judges other people. The borderline between facts and the general inferences drawn from them in respect of a group (stigmatisation) becomes indistinct and sometimes disappears. Frustration arises from the working environment, the resources available and the pressure of work. The judicial follow-up to police interventions (public prosecutor's office) is often inadequate.

Readiness to undergo the information programme is in itself a sign of determination to learn to mix with immigrants.

Some participants find the information sessions very interesting although they are not of direct use in problem situations. We nevertheless find that the information sessions have a clarifying effect when conflict situations are discussed in sessions with a more practical focus.

The contact day, consisting of a visit to a mosque, a youth centre and an association, is the ideal opportunity to compare theory with practice. Time is taken for amicable discussion of the lack of understanding and of mutual frustrations. Another significant aspect is the possibility of swapping information on their work.

In certain municipalities the information programme on immigrants was interpreted as "working with criminal immigrants".This was especially so in predominantly rural municipalities with few immigrants among their population. There are also the larger towns where police and gendarmerie officers are generally confronted with none but "negative" immigrants.

A 25 hour programme cannot provide ready-made answers to these difficult questions, especially considering that fundamental solutions often call for an educational approach geared to social problems in which emphasis must be placed on prevention rather than on mere penalisation.

Certain solutions moreover require combined work by different agencies. It is unrealistic to rely entirely on the police authorities.

Conclusions, proposals and prospects

In general, the information programme is positively assessed by participants and local authorities.

As regard police duties, the following action should be envisaged:

-       After basic training, provision of the necessary time for regular refresher retraining.

- General upgrading of the profession (including its financing) would be beneficial to the force and to the population (more selective recruitment); every municipality with a large number of immigrants should have "specialists on immigrants".

- The police force should be a reflection of society, ie it should include persons of foreign origin.

- Consultation bodies should be set up:

i. Between the various local services to have a better idea of one another's functions. This benefits not only immigrants but the population as a whole.

ii. Between the local services and the immigration sector; this aspect can be important in guarding against difficult unforeseen circumstances and working to greater preventive effect.

iii. Between the local services and the youth welfare sector as a whole.

The mandate of the Royal Commission on Migrant Policy ends in March 1993. Negotiations are currently in hand at government level to establish a "Centre for Ethnic Equality" which might take over certain functions of the Royal Commission, possibly including training and information[3]. This will nevertheless require investment to ensure that the project receives more thorough follow-up and evaluation.

The future Centre for Ethnic Equality should devise a system to cater for migrants in the same way as the present Belgian target group.

It is our duty to meet the public's aspirations for the furtherance of mutual communication and integration.

Houssein Boukhriss

---

[3]   This Centre has since been established.

2. Police School, Denmark

History

The basis, in Denmark, for the establishment of a specialist course designated "*Police activities towards and among aliens*" was the adoption of a new Aliens Act, which took effect in 1984. At the same time a Directorate for Aliens was established, and the section under the National Commissioner's Office which was responsible for aliens control (*Tilsynet med udloendinge*) was disbanded.

A new *Aliens division* (*Den Centrale Politiafdeling*) was then established under the National Commissioner's "E" Department. The Division was charged with performing a number of central policing functions and providing national assistance to the police districts throughout the country.

The Aliens Division had to perform a number of unforeseen tasks in connection with the influx into Denmark of refugees.

The work performed by the Division was hampered by the widespread public interest in refugee issues, by the ways in which these issues were treated by the media, by the need for a uniform approach in all police districts as well as by the somewhat vacillating attitude among politicians, over the years, towards the country's policy.

Therefore, the chief of the Aliens Division, raised the issue with the Director of the Danish Police School and Staff College as to whether a *one-week course* could be established, *designed to provide Division personnel with a broader basis for their job performance.*

The objective was **not** to train course members to perform casework.

Policy context

The course affected other courses provided by the Police School. The Basic Training programme saw changes in the subjects Civil Law, Psychology and Police Theory. Within the individual police districts the issue was discussed in the framework of the so-called SSP co-operation scheme (Schools, Social service and Police).

The basic aim is to acquire knowledge and an improved understanding of migrants. Knowledge and improved understanding will lead to the possibility of behavioural change - and this is the ultimate objective.

Objectives

The course aimed to provide information on the new tasks performed by police - and to provide an opportunity to discuss political aspects of aliens legislation.

Moreover, it sought to identify and illustrate differences in the administration of cases dealt with by the Aliens Division and those falling within the purview of criminal justice procedures. Course members were required to achieve an understanding of the fact that they formed a part of an administration which was essentially dissimilar from traditional police work of the investigation of crimes.

Another aim was to provide information on the differences between Danish cultural patterns and aliens' cultural backgrounds - primarily those of refugees.

Furthermore, it was to provide guidance on the language barriers which have to be overcome - not least when communication is carried out through interpreters.

The course also gave an introduction to the organisations which work with the reception and integration of refugees, such as the Danish Red Cross and the Danish Refugee Council.

This composition of subjects was supposed to provide police officers with a wider understanding of current legislation, of their co-operation partners as well as of aliens.

Course curriculum

The selection of subjects was to cover a broad perspective with an emphasis on information on migrants, in particular refugees.

Subjects chosen as course contents were - and still are:

- Introduction and the Aliens Act;

- Meeting of cultures (course conducted by an ethnographer and a psychologist);

- Integration (course members work with theories and experiences concerning dissimilar cultures and their integration (this subject will be conducted by an ethnographer);

- Danish civilization (course conducted by an ethnographer);

- International "hotbeds" (the subject is given by Foreign office officials or by academic or journalistic experts).

Documentation

Briefing on available sources of information - for use in daily work and on the longer term - on the background of aliens.

Special topic

"Islam and fundamentalism". The subject will cut across issues and will be chosen so as to provide members with an understanding of some cultural, social, political or religious driving forces which transcend nationalism. This subject is done by experts, who present Islam as a comprehensive religious system and philosophy.

Panel

The intention is to introduce the partners from the organisations with which the police co-operate, to hear their views and to exchange queries and comments between panel and course members.

Interviewing

The psychology of interviewing, with a special view to transcending cultural differences.

Interpreting

Course members will be introduced to a number of issues and problems in connection with the functions of interpreting and interpreters in police work.

Casework system

A presentation will be given on the entire casework process - of which the police form a part.

End-of-course

Review and evaluation.

Methods and materials

No "approved methods and materials" have been developed. Successive course members' knowledge and awareness will provide the starting point. Successive instructors will contribute their knowledge and views to a given subject.

The methodological aspect derives from the fact that the instructors are not employed within the police service or within affiliated institutions. More often than not they will address the issues from perspectives which are at variance with common opinions among police officers. This is what is intended: to break with police officers' accustomed norms and ideas.

Participants/client group

The first course members were selected among the personnel of the Aliens Division. It is intended that the course shall be taken by all police officers in connection with their attendance on the compulsory further training courses.

Staffing

Today, the Police School is responsible for the contents and implementation of these courses. Day-to-day management rests with a Section or Unit Leader who liaises with course lecturers/instructors.

Evaluation

Each course will be evaluated by course members and instructors. After every three courses a comparative study of the evaluations will be undertaken and new trends - in a political context as well as for policing - in society will be reviewed.

The course programme has started better than anticipated. Many police officers experienced a spiritual "eye-opener" - revealing a lack of understanding of aliens, various prejudices, superstitions and so forth.

A problem which remains for the future concerns the feasibility of having *every* Danish police officer attend courses of this nature within a reasonable time. Another problem, which is an administrative one, though, concerns the coordination of courses on a topic which changes so rapidly and is so sensitive.

The Danish Police School is planning to incorporate special instruction in Human Rights delivered by the International Rehabilitation and Research Centre for Victims of Torture (*R.C.T.*), which is a non-governmental institute.

The major problem outside police training is to encourage various well-intentioned groups, migrants, citizens and social agencies to enter into constructive co-operation. Here, the above-mentioned SSP co-operation scheme will be of profound importance. Juvenile gangs and rising unemployment, which will often befall migrants and ruin their accustomed family patterns, are issues towards which the police will have to direct preventive efforts. And they are issues which will make increasing demands on modern police training and on police officers of all ranks.

Arne Thomsen

3. Police School, Finland

History

The basic police training concerning **foreigners** (*the word refers here to any person who is not a citizen of Finland*) has traditionally included two elements:

a.   law education regarding the principles of the Aliens' Act and its effects on police work by a representative of the Ministry of Interior;

b.   the subject of ethnic relations included in the lectures on ethics within the psychology course (with particular reference to the culture of the gypsies, as an example of a minority group). The main objective has been to stress the fact that all citizens are to be treated equally.

However, in the 1980's the training has changed due to the fact that aliens have began to arrive in Finland at a slowly but steadily increasing rate. In 1989 the Office for Aliens' Affairs was separated from the Police Office in the Ministry of the Interior. The new Aliens' Act and Decree was issued at the beginning of 1991.

Context of the policy

The new Aliens' Act and the **Defoir**-project of the Nordic Police Schools and Colleges (1988-89) (see section I.10 below for further details) led to a reorganization of the training concerning foreigners at the Police School.

Objectives

The *objectives* of the training are as follows:

1.   police officers must be well acquainted with the Act;

2.   they must be able to put into practice the principle of treating all people in an equal and professional way;

3.   they must have a practical command of English relevant to the situations where they meet foreigners.

Curriculum of the courses

Two basic courses are planned at the Police School:

During the first 12-month course students are taught the primary skills and knowledge of police work. After having completed at least one year's practical training as constables, students return for the second, more extensive basic course lasting for five months.

In the both basic courses lectures on the Aliens' Act and its practical effects on police work are given by a superintendent. The person concerned has been involved in questions concerning foreigners for quite a considerable period since he occupies a post at Helsinki-Vantaa Airport.

As far as the teaching of psychology is concerned, the course consists of the main concepts of ethics and general recommendations. Furthermore, there are lectures on minority cultures (e.g. that of the gypsies) and some psychological concepts like xenophobia, attitudes and stereotypes.

The *Police College in Espoo* arranges two different types of training concerning foreigners. The police officers of higher rank are given regular lessons there which include social psychological topics together with a two-day seminar about issues concerning foreigners. The seminar is supervised by the college's psychology lecturer, Lasse Nurmi.

Furthermore, for those police officers who are regularly in contact with foreigners in their work, special two-week courses are available. They are directed especially to police officers who work as trainers for their colleagues and also to those whose entire duties are concerned with foreigners' affairs.

Participants

Both at the Police School and at the College *all students take part in the training*. The only exceptions are those college courses mentioned above, which are aimed at special categories of participant.

Composition of the planning teams

The participants in the **Defoir**-project are mainly responsible for the planning of the training courses. There is also a special group of officials in the Ministry of the Interior who work out plans for the short training courses. As a rule, the instructors and the other staff are employed by the police organisation but officials from other organisations, as well as foreigners themselves, have also been called on to participate as guest lecturers.

Evaluation

The development of these training activities has demonstrated that police constables must master the basic concepts and understanding of the work concerning foreigners before they are able to discuss

65

issues arising from foreigners' affairs and to adopt a way of thinking about these questions which is free from emotional interference; only then it will be possible for them to fulfil their duties in the manner assumed by the law.

Erkki Ellonen

4. National Police Study and Training Centre, France

The "Centre National d'Etudes et de Formation" (CNEF) - responsible principally for in-service training for police officers - has taken three major training initiatives in the area of police/immigrant relations.

Back in 1983, the **National Police Training Charter** set out 12 aims and two of these aims concern problems of police officer training in their relations with immigrants.

-       Aim N° 5 *"Fostering better understanding between police officers and the public"*

-       Aim N° 7 *"Enabling police officers to analyze social factors".*

A number of measures recommended in connection with the latter aim included "in all departments, encouraging the holding of meetings or round tables with members of society concerned by police activity : the general public, those who work with the police, special communities, etc."

In 1989, in the wake of an assessment of this training policy, a "training contract" covering several years was prepared and is now being implemented. It reiterates the need for "the police in towns and cities to be partners in everyday life", and to that end Aim N° 2 ("Giving the police the means both to contribute actively to social control and to use all available partnership resources") also lays down two measures:

-       Improving public relations;
-       Promoting initiatives to improve understanding of social phenomena.

Summer schools

At the summer schools, police officers and teachers spend about a week looking together at a problem they have in common (usually teenagers or the family). In 1988, participants tackled the question "Towards a multi-cultural society", taking as their example the Minguettes district of Vénissieux (near Lyon).

The same question was studied at the 1989 summer school, the theme being "Immigrant families".

In 1990, when the French police training sub-directorate asked the CNEF to help increase the number of summer schools and decentralise them, the theme "Teenagers and Immigration" seemed the obvious choice as the main subject of a working discussion week in Marseille together with the Regional Delegation for Recruitment and Training. 400 copies of the proceedings were subsequently published and distributed to all departments.

In 1991, using the same set-up, police officers and teachers spent a week-long course on the narrower subject of "Teenagers in France and North Africa".

In August 1992, the CNEF took charge of the summer school and examined "The integration or exclusion of young people in France and Europe".

A special in-service training course: "Cultures and Cultural Differences"

The second major initiative taken by the CNEF dates from the last quarter of 1991 when it launched a course entitled "Cultures and Cultural Differences", targeted exclusively at police officers and held under an agreement with the ADRI (Agence de Développement des Relations Interculturelles - Inter-cultural relations development agency) and we are considering whether this should be developed and a similar course be held in 1993.

A seminar held at Gif on 2 October 1991: "Teenagers and Immigration"

The "Rencontres de Gif" are seminars on various social themes, bringing together all representatives of institutions and voluntary bodies concerned by the particular problem. On 2 October 1991, 150 people, including 50 police officers, attended the seminar on the subject of "Teenagers and Immigration".

Aims

The aims of the summer schools

a.   The aim of the first summer school on "Teenagers and Immigration" was to study to what extent, social background being equal, young people of immigrant origin encounter greater difficulties at school or work than their French contemporaries.

b.   The second summer school on "Teenagers in France and North Africa" set out to study the behaviour and social and occupational integration of young people both in France (young Frenchmen) and in Morocco, Algeria and Tunisia. This study took as its premise the existence of features common to all young people, eg similar behaviour patterns or difficulties of integration in society and the working environment linked to social background or local economic circumstances.

c.   The third summer school, on "The integration or exclusion of young people in France and Europe", sought answers to the following questions:

-      Are the problems of integration or exclusion in France and Europe peculiar to young people of foreign origin, or are they faced by all young people from underprivileged social classes?

-      How do the processes of integration or exclusion function?

These aims were selected because of the lack of understanding by police officers of the problems these young people encounter. This can often lead in turn to stigmatisation of such young people and their frequent categorisation as overwhelmingly delinquent. Studying these phenomena in their socio-economic or even political context, can lead to a reappraisal and police officers can be encouraged to change their attitude towards these young people.

The course on "Cultures and Cultural Differences"

The main purpose of the course was:

- to offer a first-time approach to the cultural realities of immigration from north and black Africa and south-east Asia;

- to afford police officers a better understanding of communication situations among peoples from different cultural backgrounds.

It should be explained to police officers that certain types of behaviour, expressions or gestures are not meant to be aggressive or offensive.

The Gif seminar on "Teenagers and Immigration"

This meeting was intended to allow representatives of various institutions and associations to compare their perceptions of young people of foreign origin and their ways of dealing with them, and to study both contemporary research on the subject and the policy adopted by the Department of Integration.

Many of the participants "were unaware of the thrust of policy in this field, what it had actually achieved on the ground and the successes it had scored". This seminar was also intended to reveal to those who work with the police what consideration had been given to the matter by police officers themselves.

Programme

1.   Summer schools

Week-long programmes, prepared by universities and researchers, including afternoon working groups and field visits.

2.   Course on "Cultures and Cultural Differences"

It comprised three two-day modules, once a month, each of which concentrated on a single immigrant community.

3.   Gif seminar on "Teenagers and Immigration"

This was a one-day seminar. The programme included a demographic, legal and social approach to the phenomenon of immigration, plus an original paper delivered by an academic whose analysis of autobiographical novels written by young people of north African origin had enabled him to study their relationships with their families and their root culture.

Over 150 persons took part, including 50 police officers (40 % constables, 30 % sergeants, 15 % inspectors (plain clothes), 10 % officers, 5 % superintendents) and 100 others (70 % State education staff, 20 % legal service staff, 10 % others (elected representatives, local and regional authority staff, social workers).

Methods

At the summer schools and on the training course the real-life experience of the trainees was exploited. Rather than papering over cultural differences with humanist talk, it was decided tackle them on the basis of the practical experience of those actually involved.

Teaching staff

1. At summer schools

The courses were taught by university staff, people in charge of associations for immigrants or working with them, and other professionals (police department and judiciary staff).

2. On the training course

The ADRI (Agence de Développement des Relations Interculturelles) and its team of university researchers offered their services.

3. At the Gif seminar

Most of the instruction was given by institutional representatives: from the INSEE, from the Interministerial Department of Urban Affairs, from the State education system and from the Department of Immigration; a university teacher also took part.

Assessment

An overall assessment was carried out but only in the case of the summer schools and the CNEF training course.

1. Assessment of the summer schools

The trainees generally felt that attendance had improved their understanding of the problems of immigration and would be useful in their work; they also felt personally enriched.

Bringing together professionals from different institutions can only heighten awareness of immigrant problems. Not only can they compare notes with academics and researchers, but they can continually share ideas with fellow professionals, thus enabling a sometimes corporatist view of problems to be reassessed.

The training course

The two main aims of attending this course were put into words by one of the trainees:

- "to understand the integration potential and difficulties of the three types of immigrant community in France",

- "to come to grips with the cultural characteristics of these social groups".

Participants were unanimous that the training course had been tailor-made for them professionally.

What lessons can be drawn from these experiences?

Except for those officials who are in permanent contact with the immigrant communities (eg those working at special counters), trainees want an extremely pragmatic approach. Talk about the cultural richness of these communities is pointless unless the real-life problems encountered by police officers dealing with the phenomena of urban violence are catered for.

Their remarks and ideas ought to be taken on board and put into perspective so that another approach may gradually be developed.

Daniel Bellet

5. Police College
Berlin, Germany

After the unification of the two German states, and the collapse of the communist systems in Central and Eastern Europe, Berlin increasingly recovered its traditional role as metropolis between East and West.

Opening of the borders to neighbouring Eastern and Western European countries in connection with a dramatic difference in prosperity between these countries led to increasing migration movements to the city of Berlin. Thus, the number of foreigners living in Berlin rose by about 12 000 persons between 30 June 1992 and 31 December 1992 and is steadily climbing. On 30 June 1992, Berlin registered 366 553 foreigners totalling 10,6 per cent of the entire population.

Since the fall of the wall, the Berlin Police Force faces a special challenge in exercising jurisdiction for the entire city with the take-over of 9 600 members on 1 October 1990, formerly belonging to the people's police.

For the "Police Training" section of the Berlin Police Department this means that alongside the regular training, originally designed for West-Berlin police officers only, they now also have to prepare the newcomers for their service in a multi-ethnic, pluralistic society. Our activities stress the term tolerance in the sense of having a liberal attitude.

This is achieved at social events between police officers and foreigners of different origin and serves to foster understanding for other cultures, their way of life and the special problems that may arise for foreigners. The activities mentioned are carried out in co-operation with, and with the support of, the Commissioner for Aliens Affairs of the Berlin Senate.

History/Policy context

The working group "foreigners" (AGA) began to offer training courses for the service in areas of alien concentration already shortly after its establishment in 1971.

Due to the high proportion of Turkish nationals amongst the foreigners living in Berlin, it was considered sensible, in the interests of more effective police work, to teach officers the Turkish mentality, this being one way of avoiding conflicts right from the start. Furthermore, it was of importance to instruct members of the uniformed police on aliens affairs thus developing a "snowball effect" among uniformed officers. AGA-officers now also transmit basic knowledge to members of the former "people's police" thereby focusing on the origin, structure, and mentality of the alien groups living in Berlin.

Police officers being trained on the middle service level experienced a new structure in 1988. Up to this time the topic had been included in the curriculum under Public and Constitutional Law, Political Science, and History. The subjects "foreigners" and "migrants and ethnic relations" were taught during the first and second years of training under the focal point of "mankind, minorities, nations, society, and the state and its elements".

In connection with intensified efforts by the Berlin Senate for a better integration policy, Turkish nationals were accepted as police trainees for the first time in 1988. They are obliged to acquire German citizenship at the end of their training period which is now of three years. Ever since this time, the topic is no longer dealt with on a theoretical basis only.

The Police College and the "Political Science" sections in co-operation with the Commissioner for Aliens Affairs of the Berlin Senate, and also AGA-officers organized meetings for panel-discussions between trainees and young aliens which additionally included visits to Turkish mosques and sports events. Moreover, since September 1989, trainees of the middle service level have had to attend 4-week workshops entitled "behaviour training". With the aid of sketches on the topics "questions of prejudice" and "behaviour and rituals of special ethnic and religious groups" this domain is questioned, also from the psychological point of view. "Behaviour training" is also offered in a continuation course which at present is attended mainly by officers belonging to the so-called closed units (Special Forces).

The number of asylum seekers has increased greatly in the past years and is making the headlines everywhere.

It was only in 1990 that the "Political Science" section introduced to its trainees one-day visits to homes of asylum-seekers. In 1991 these visits were extended to *all* trainees in their first year of training, with the idea of maintaining close contacts with foreigners and being given the opportunity to talk with social workers and the inhabitants of the homes. The officers may also decide they wish to spend their obligatory three-week social-practical in one of these homes.

The topic on "*foreigners in Berlin - migration movements*" also constitutes a main field for training for the service on both middle and higher level and for the uniformed and the plain clothes police. Next to transfer of knowledge and discussion about practical police experience, emphasis is increasingly placed on immediate contact with foreigners. For instance, officers attending a group leader training course with subsequent responsibilities at middle service level are invited to discussions with the Commissioner for Aliens Affairs after having heard lectures on political science. Again this is followed up by a visit to a home for asylum seekers.

Since 1989 the "Political Science" section has offered training courses for criminal investigators. The one-day workshop, consisting of 15 officers each time, includes current socio-political questions. In the past months, the role of ethnic groups and other minorities in our society was discussed. Representatives of foreigners living in our city and representatives of the Commissioner for Aliens Affairs are invited to these workshops.

The Berlin Police offers several initiatives/courses. The *aims* are all similar in their attempt to allow participants:

-   to understand the meaning of international law (Geneva Convention on refugee questions);

-   to obtain information on the constitutional state in the Federal Republic of Germany, on its aliens and asylum procedural law, and the political discussion thereof;

-   to learn about the development of foreign populations in Germany and Berlin and their ethnic structures;

-   to distinguish between the terms "foreigner", "guest worker", "asylum seeker", and "refugee";

-   to understand the reason for migration and its international ramifications;

-   to learn to do daily police work more effectively by acquiring knowledge about differences in mentality, thereby avoiding conflicts;

-   to diminish prejudice through direct contact, discussions and mutual activities (sports events) with foreigners;

-   to learn to avoid stereotyping with respect to criminal behaviour by foreigners.

Unfortunately, it has become obvious lately that police officers have pre-conceptions and even prejudices against foreigners. They are concerned that it will become more difficult to resolve the rising social problems after unification and to adapt to living together with an increasing number of foreigners. The required political concessions and decisions of principle concerning foreigners are still lacking. Consequently, in training courses it has to be demonstrated that "simple solutions" as propagated by radical political parties are no real solution to the problem. Especially for the members of the former "people's police" it is important to understand that many-sided problems in a pluralistic society have to be openly debated.

Methods and materials

A topic may be illustrated by the trainer either with the aid of a video film or slides or as a lecture which then has to be commented on by the participants. One section also includes sketches in their "behaviour-training" which are filmed and evaluated afterwards by the group. The "Political Science" section elaborated a circular letter on the topic "foreigners in Berlin" which is available to each police officer. Furthermore, data made available by the Landeszentrale für Politische Bildungsarbeit (Central office for political education in Berlin) and the Commissioner for aliens affairs is used. Current events are presented on slides and on video film.

Participants/Client group

One main field of activities is the training of uniformed police officers of the middle service level. They receive a three-year training and are aged between 16 and 34 years. After completion of their training they are primarily transferred to the closed units or serve as patrol officers at police stations. The training courses are designed to give these officers further preparation for their duty in a multi-ethnic society.

Training on the higher service level for uniformed and plain clothes police officers as well as the trade supervisory service is carried out at the Higher College in Berlin. Again, it requires three years of studies.

At present, training courses are offered to members of the closed units, auxiliary police officers, and criminal investigators as well as officers attending a group leader training course.

It is intended, however, to renew this offer in 1994 for all police members.

The staff consists primarily of officers from the higher service level of both branches, i.e. uniformed and plain clothes police, who graduated from a higher technical college after three years of study.

The Sociological Service of the Berlin Police employs psychologists; "behaviour-training" is carried out by both teachers and psychologists. The "Political Science" section invites external experts to its classes, e.g. social workers, sociologists and representatives of different foreigners associations, and thereby tries to avoid that topics are treated one-sidedly, merely from a police point of view.

The *AGA-staff* have long-term experience with foreigners and close contact with religious and social establishments and are thus able to include representatives of these organizations in their educational work.

Evaluation

Trainers and participants together evaluate the subject material and in general it is accepted with interest. In particular, the discussions with external experts are very much in demand.

Visits to the homes of asylum seekers require extensive and careful preparation. When these visits were first introduced, some officers had apprehensions resulting from unfortunate meetings with inhabitants of such homes on other official occasions (e.g. official search). These officers were the ones who changed their minds after returning from our excursions. They admitted they had successfully broadened their mental horizon and did not regard the issue solely from a police point of view any longer.

Other sections within the Berlin Police Force are taking steps to improve relationships with foreigners. For instance, work groups combatting youth violence (sub-sections against group-violence and prevention of violence), have established reciprocal contacts. A police project "kick-sport" against youth delinquency seeks to develop co-operation between police, social workers and young athletes. It attracts by many young foreigners.

Final remarks

To avoid hostile manifestations against foreigners, political decisions are urgently needed. Police shall protect the life and dignity of each person living in Germany. The developed activities in the training courses shall contribute to a better understanding of foreigners and their way of life in our society.

Eckhardt Lazai

6. Office for Multicultural Affairs Frankfurt/Main, Germany

1.   Introduction

It is not only since xenophobia in Germany started again during the last year, that the role of the police in a multi-ethnic society is being discussed. Numerous complaints about racial prejudices and racially motivated misconduct of police officers reached the Office of Multicultural Affairs in Frankfurt/Main. These are the letters of migrants (asylum seeking) refugees, complaints of the schools and of several associations of foreigners. All together the incidents indicate that there are problems in the contact between the police and people of foreign origin. In some cases police officers behave in an aggressive manner towards migrants and refugees. In other cases there is the deliberate overlooking of crimes committed against foreigners. The problems result from various conflicts and especially in city quarters with a high crime-rate. A latent antipathy against people of foreign origin must be supposed in all parts of the police. Xenophobic attitudes occur in trainees as well as in uniformed officers and detective inspectors.

This is the background upon which the Office of Multicultural Affairs has started to conceptualise a discrimination awareness training. The Office is considering diverse actions, although it is yet unclear which of them will be realized. This depends largely on the acceptance by the police. Moreover, there is the question of financial, personal and political support.

2.   The situation in Frankfurt/Main and Hessen

The discussion about xenophobia within the Frankfurt Police Force started in October 1991. The reason was that a pamphlet of racist contents was found at several police stations, and also in the police headquarters. It is still unclear, if the pamphlet was written and distributed by police officers or if other persons outside the Force intended to defame police activities.

However, this incident started the discussion about xenophobia within the Frankfurt Police. The Minister of the Interior of Hessen, Herbert Guenter, asked the police officers to speak about this issue. The police union made a seminar about xenophobia and the theatre group at the police college in Wiesbaden staged a play on anti-racism. While in Frankfurt the dialogue and the sensitization began, another town in Hessen, Giessen, made a first step to institutionalize the chance for foreigners to complain about discrimination: the police established 10 confidential persons who can be contacted by victims of racism and by foreigners, particularly women, who might be afraid of other police officers. These persons are also responsible for identifying xenophobic tendencies within the police force and informing their colleagues. This means that the police have to take a critical view towards the statistics of crimes committed by foreigners.

The actual police statistics show that foreigners are more likely to be criminal than Germans. But nevertheless, one cannot conclude that the question of criminality, especially of high-violent crimes, is a typical question of non-German citizens: as they do not specify the different groups of foreign delinquents in detail, in this respect the statistics are inaccurate and insufficient.

3.   The political context

As the number of assaults on refugee hostels increases, as racist attacks towards foreigners become more and more brutal and as migrants - including all people who look like foreigners - do not feel safe, the question results about the role of the police in combating xenophobia by carefully directed measures. On the one hand, it is evident that the police cannot tolerate the violence of right-wing groups. On the other hand, one cannot expect that the police solve political and social problems. When in Rostock 200 right-wing extremists attacked and then set fire to a foreigners' hostel under the applause of several

84

thousand bystanders, this expressed xenophobia as well as protest against political failure. At the present time the police feel themselves as scapegoat. They are criticised by the population, by the politicians and by foreigners.

The police has still not found their identity in a multi-ethnic society. In order to do so, one has to look for new issues irrespective of the present role as fire-brigade for acute incendiarism. A long-term perspective is in urgent demand.

4. Police training

4.1. The urgent requirements of anti-racism training

It is obvious that in the German democratic system racist behaviour and attitudes of police officers are illegal. Nevertheless, the above mentioned complaints show that people of foreign origin and ethnic minorities feel discriminated against by the police. However, since the pamphlet-incident in Frankfurt the professional and private discrimination against police officers have increased as well. Now, they might be shouted at as racists and right-wing extremists more often than before. Foreigners as well as police officers should give up their vice-versa reservations.

In the long run the conflict management in every individual case will be no solution. One must kindle a consciousness for discrimination in general, because prevention is more effective than intervention. In a multi-ethnic society it is the police duty to prevent and to combat racially motivated behaviour. Besides, the police need the foreigners' willingness to report and to testify. For the tasks in a multi-ethnic society the police are not well-enough prepared, yet.

4.2. Aims

The following topics need to be covered:

Behaviour

- how to find strategies in order to prevent or solve conflicts in problem situations with foreigners;

- the ability to analyse these conflicts with regard to their origin (misunderstandings, language problems, etc.);

- the ability to communicate effectively with migrants on the telephone;

- the ability to look for what is immediately required in a situation instead of behaving in a routine manner;

- the ability to identify and reject discriminatory behaviour among colleagues.

Attitudes

- awareness for prejudices concerning social and ethnic minorities, discriminatory attitudes and beliefs;

- identification with the role of the helper, also for people of foreign origin.

Cognition

- knowledge about the lifestyle of foreigners in Germany and other countries;

- knowledge about culture-specific ways to live, to behave and to think;

-   enlargement of knowledge about politics and law concerning foreigners.

Motivation

-   interest in foreign countries and their people;

-   the readiness to reflect on xenophobia in the further private and professional life and to learn from mistakes and misunderstandings;

-   interest in institutional changes and commitment.

4.3.   Concept

The concept suggests creating discrimination awareness by focusing on the personal experiences with discrimination by police officers. It can be assumed that there might be established an emotional link between their personal feelings and those of other people.

Four steps are to be distinguished:

1.   *Discrimination awareness*: Exchange of discrimination experiences concerning the person itself (no personal liberty in choosing the police station; bad payment, etc.); collection, classification, consequences and development of prejudices; finding answers to the questions: How does a victim of discrimination feel? What can be done against it?; an analysis of the conflicts that the police officers experienced with people of foreign origin.

2.   *Extension of behaviour skills by role-plays that are conceptualised close to the actual situation*: The simulation includes incidents in which people belonging to ethnic or social minorities are victims or perpetrators of crimes. Also the conflict management with xenophobic Germans has to be trained.

3.　　*Information*: for instance reports on the situation of foreigners in Germany; discussions about foreign policy and foreign law; sensitization for culture-specific behaviour and thinking; reflection about typically German attitudes, habits, etc.

4.　　*Establishment of long-term contact between the police and people of foreign origin*: The dialogue with persons from other cultures is to be actively searched and the experiences should be seen as a great opportunity for the personal and social development. This means for example that police officers visit an asylum seekers' hostel or make a symposium in which delegates of different cultural backgrounds might discuss problems and issues.

The scientific basis of this concept is a psychoanalytic view of how discrimination develops. Prejudices result from the projection of the person's own characteristics, wishes and fears on weaker helpless people. Racism cannot be separated from sexism, anti-Semitism and the discrimination against social minorities like homosexuals, homeless persons, handicapped people, women and men from the former East Germany and people with speech impediments. Policewomen may play a key role in the decrease of racist behaviour. Because of their own discrimination experiences they might be more sensitive towards prejudices and unfair behaviour to minorities than police*men*. If racism, sexism and other forms of discrimination are not taken into consideration at the same time, there is the risk of curing isolated symptoms without considering the whole body.

4.4.　Methods

A 3-hour workshop and a one-day training are conceptualised as preparation for a 1 or 2 week course. The trainer team consists of social scientists and police officers with profound experience in their professional and private lives. In small groups with about 10 persons the seminar participants exercise role-plays (with video-feedback), communicate on the telephone, watch films, discuss current topics, exchange their problems and opinions, listen to reports.

4.5   Problems

On the one hand, the anti-racism seminars must be short because of the severe shortage of personnel. On the other hand, according to the psychoanalytic theory, there has to be enough time to mention all kinds of discrimination, including personal experiences. Otherwise the seminars run the risk to reinforce prejudices or to result in a personal breakdown.

Another difficulty is how to focus on several forms of discrimination in one seminar. Perhaps the police officers prefer the emphasis on the behaviour towards social minorities rather than ethnic groups. In such a conflict the trainer must find an adequate solution corresponding to the need in an actual situation.

Problems should to be identified and analysed in regular, systematic evaluations.

5.   Other measures

- The planned discrimination awareness training also has the aim to increase the acceptance of colleagues who are from different cultural origins. Unfortunately, in Frankfurt/Main only people with German citizenship are allowed to enter the police force. This ought to change in the future - a task for German politicians.

- In a working group called "Police in Discussion" initiatives for the employment of foreigner in the police might be taken. There, room could be found for conflicts between the police and citizens. The group would also be responsible for searching for further strategies in order to improve the contact between the police and minorities.

- More detailed police statistics on crime will have to be established with a new category added for racial violence and threats.

-    In police stations posters which ask foreigners in different languages to report on xenophobic crimes are to be hung up.

-    Reports in the mass media about the role of the police in today's society could be analysed and evaluated.

-    The anti-discrimination seminar should be regarded as part of the whole training programme concerning communication, conflict and stress management.

6.   Conclusion

The context and contents of police training concerning migrants and ethnic relations indicate that even if a police officer is in most cases not a politician, he can and must contribute to the fight against xenophobia. Training the consciousness for this responsibility requires a certain organizational context including political support and social changes. Seeking to intensify the contact and to solve the conflicts between the German police forces and people of foreign origin remains an unavoidable challenge for the future.

Bettina Franzke

7. Police Study Centre, Netherlands

The "Indian Summer Course"

Training programme for managing positive action

During the past 40 years the Netherlands has had increasing experience with the settlement of migrant workers and refugees, but around 1980 this situation began to change as the economic problems in the Netherlands began to increase and it became obvious that while most of the immigrants were no longer needed on the labour market they did not want to return home. On the contrary, they demanded social and economic equality and the right to maintain their own cultural identity.

The flow of immigrants continued and signs of discrimination and racism increased, causing growing tension in Amsterdam, Utrecht, Rotterdam and The Hague.

In 1983 the Dutch Government published its first minority policy document. Its main message was that the Dutch police should become a "mirror of society" by recruiting people from among the minority groups.

In 1988 a new document was produced by the Ministry: **"The Positive Action Plan"**. The main change in approach was that the argument for positive action (the idea that you should feel guilty about the past, combined with the *principle of justice*) was redirected towards the principle of *professionalism*: the ability to deal fairly and effectively with members of minority groups. The handling of multicultural problems in society thus becomes an important issue for the management of diversity in an organisation.

In the meantime (1986-90) a special training team (*Training, Advice and Course Team*) (TACT) was asked to start up a training programme for police forces and police schools. Nevertheless, as it is difficult to link the operational level to the more strategic management level, the Ministry asked the **Police Study Centre** to develop activities designed to elicit the necessary commitment.

This was the birth of the **"Indian Summer Course"**, a training programme specially designed for managers of the transcultural process and aiming to elicit commitment at the top level.

The Indian Summer Course is built on the principle that an organisation cannot change its structure and culture without first taking the following steps:

-   there has to be a certain pressure (external or internal) for changing the present situation;

-   there has to be leadership based on a clear and inspiring vision/mission;

-   there has to be a policy strategy linked to the vision;

-   the policy strategy should be carefully implemented (preparatory action);

-   at the start, "guided action" should be used at the operational level.

If just one of these steps is not properly carried through, the process of change desired by the manager will not be successful.

The first course outlines were made by the Police Study Centre in cooperation with the **Anne Frank Foundation** and then the course was developed in more detail by Isis, the University of Utrecht, the consultancy bureau Joka Vriesema and the Police Study Centre.

The present situation is that the Anne Frank Foundation and the Police Study Centre intend to "reframe" the course to more European standards (i.e. to improve and adapt the course to different national management concepts and different cultures).

A special and very effective feature of the course is a number of "intervision days" for participants afterwards. These days are intended to carefully guide and support the steps taken in the different organisations.

At the same time the Ministry set up a working group of police managers and police trainers with the task of developing a programme of courses for the various middle-management and operational levels. The Police Study Centre takes part in this working group, which is managed by the Police District Commander of Rotterdam.

In 1992 the Police Study Centre initiated the European *Multi-Cultural Police Network* (EMCP) with the aim of keeping well informed on developments in the multi-cultural situation. The network consists of a group of police experts from Great Britain, France, Germany, Belgium and the Netherlands, who exchange experience and know-how in this field.

The objectives are regular information exchange, building up a collection of relevant documents, forming a close support network.

A.C. Buitenhuis

8. Anne Frank Centre Netherlands

Dutch Police and equal opportunities

"To become a multi-racial police force has to be seen as a survival strategy for the police"

(Commissioner of the Rotterdam Police Force)

An ethnically diverse police organisation is necessary for its representativeness and its acceptability in society. The police organisation has a multi-ethnic "clientele", so police professionalism requires the ability to deal fairly and effectively with people of different ethnic origins. The police as an employer can contribute in a positive way in dealing with the problem of disproportionate unemployment among members of ethnic minority groups.

Around the time that the Dutch Government's main policy document on ethnic minorities was being prepared (1983), Lord Scarman's report on the confrontations in London between the police and black youths in particular was published. The report emphasised the importance of recruiting and appointing police officers from ethnic minorities.

The police forces of the four big cities (Amsterdam, Rotterdam, Utrecht and The Hague), supported by the Ministry of Home Affairs (Directorate of Police), began to aim at a more representative police force.

Something had to be done to adapt the system. This had implications for recruitment, selection, training and supervision but it was difficult to translate good intentions into policy. The drop-out percentage of members of ethnic groups appeared to be significantly higher than that of whites in every phase of the process of joining the police force.

The Anne Frank Centre

In 1986 the Ministry of Home Affairs asked the **Anne Frank Centre** to provide training inputs and consultancy in the area of equal opportunities within the Dutch police forces. The **Anne Frank Centre** formed a multi-ethnic and multi-disciplinary Training, Advice and Course Team (TACT) which, since then, has organised about 100 three-day training sessions. In 1990 TACT had completed the training of:

- staffs of police training schools;
- mentors (probationer tutors);
- recruiting staff;
- selection staff;
- middle management (sergeants and inspectors).

In 1988 the TACT group helped initiate the "Indian Summer" Course of the Police Study Centre. Since 1990, the **Anne Frank Centre** has, on request, provided assistance to individual police forces.

Of course the police should be trained in better ways of dealing with the problems arising in a multi-ethnic society, in managing diversity and the (professional) consequences of serving in a police force for a multi-ethnic society. But structural relations can only be improved if training activities are integrated into "police policy", backed up by a "political policy". Training has to become a normal part of professionalisation. It must be inclusive and be approached from a multi-ethnic perspective.

The **Anne Frank Centre** tries to integrate equal opportunity policies into the areas of personnel management, human resource management and the adaptation of existing training programmes. In other words, into the mainstream, "normal" practice of the organisations.

Training activities from 1986 to 1990

1. Recruitment and selection

Everyone who wishes to join the police force and meets the requirements has to be tested at the National Selection Centre.

In recent years the examination materials and methods have been revised and "black" expertise has been brought in. The selection centre's current experiments with assessment methods are giving hopeful results. The idea in this case is that it should not be a question of lowering standards and criteria, but of shifting them.

After the selection tests applicants undergo a background and experience investigation. Interviews with parents, relatives, former employers, teachers, etc take place. The professionals conducting such interviews also have to be trained, and this is already partly completed.

2. Schooling

Most regional police training schools have experience with ethnic diversity. The policy should aim at better prospects for more black students to undergo adequate training: adequate for the future execution of their job, but also adapted to the potential, wishes and needs of the students. The problem we face is that there is still no complete and integrated policy on management of and education for diversity and not everyone concerned with schooling is willing to foster institutional adaptations.

The consequences of, and also the resistance against, a multi-ethnic policy are too seldom points of discussion by the management. Attention to ethnic groups is often incidental and little time is devoted to it.

The educational material is hardly adapted to a multi-ethnic society and sometimes openly reinforces prejudices. The class material, tests and assessments are often needlessly complicated and presuppose that members of ethnic groups possess advanced "white" knowledge.

Since our training and consultancy period, a lot of this material has been revised and teachers are more aware of multi-ethnicity and its consequences for police training and police work.

3. Mentoring and supervising

After the first phase of 11 months at school, a practical work period of 5 months follows in the police force where the student will eventually work.

Police students are supervised in groups by a "mentor" who, in fact, functions as a liaison officer between school and practice.

We also focused on the interaction between the mentor/teacher and student and the how it can be obstructed by presuppositions, stereotypes and prejudice. Recognition of these problems should be part of the training for such professionals and others.

4. The police force

After police training, recruits from ethnic minorities may be confronted with a work environment that is less than enthusiastic. Problems hardly ever arise in the relationship between the black constable and the public, as is sometimes thought to be the case, but mainly with colleagues. Jokes, discriminatory remarks, unwillingness to be on duty with a member of an ethnic group, insufficient backing by the sergeant and inspector, are the reasons given by too many "minority" constables for quitting the police force sooner or later.

If the atmosphere in the group on duty is "migrant-unfriendly" or sometimes even hostile, more often than not the black constable will be transferred without the group on duty ever being called to account. In such cases the management will have to adopt more explicit and effective action.

Our training mainly focused on intercultural managerial skills, inter-ethnic communication, group dynamics and assessment skills.

5.   Conclusions

The police organisations are doing a great deal to make equal opportunities policies a success.

It has now become clear that a policy of positive action should consist in more than just "opening the door". Some of the consequences of such action can be predicted but some of them cannot, which is why it is important to have a permanent feedback from inside and outside the organisation.

Another clear conclusion is that equal opportunities policies should be accompanied by training of the people concerned. Training can never replace structural measures but it can facilitate the introduction and development of change.

One of the major achievements of the past years is that it would be difficult to find any top-ranking Dutch police officer who is not aware of the interest of the organisation itself in becoming "pluriform in uniform" in order to meet the challenges of a changing society. Some forces are facing the consequences of the next phase in a process that leads from affirmative action to affirming diversity.

Implementing, developing and supporting intercultural human resource management is what the **Anne Frank Centre** is aiming at and stands for, not only in the police organisations, but in regard to (personnel) management in general.

Diversity is normal and getting the best out of a diverse labour force, recognising and developing talent, regardless of race, ethnicity or gender, is not only a matter of justice and social interest, but also a matter of economics.

Jan Van Kooten

9. The Norwegian reform in police training

The challenge of migrants and ethnic relations

The historical background and policy context

In 1985, the Norwegian parliament decided that the two-year training period of police recruits should be expanded into a three-year period and integrated into the ordinary college and university system in Norway. In 1987, a report was issued by the Ministry of Justice, but little of practical significance was actually done. In September 1990, however, a project team was established. The team's comprehensive two-volume report recommended several changes in the organisation, structure and content of the future police training in Norway.

Most of these recommendations were accepted by the Ministry and are now being implemented at the Police College in Oslo. However, the reform does not change the centralized character of Norwegian police training. The Police College remains the one and only institution of police training at all levels in Norway.

In August 1992, seven year after the decision of Parliament, the **first** class of 250 **students** embarked on their three-year journey into the police profession. The first of the three years covers theoretical and practical training at the College. As students, they are supposed to attend lectures and work group sessions, like every other student at the universities. And like every other student, they are **not** employed and paid by the State and therefore have to rely on loans to finance their studies. But most important: as students they cannot be given orders by police officers. This absence of power and authority over the learners constitutes a fundamental change in the philosophy of Norwegian police training.

The second year consists of practical service and training in the local forces (still as students), and in the third and final year, the students return to the college to complete their theoretical and practical training.

From August 1992 to June 1993, this new model of police training will co-exist with the old model. In October 1992, the students are joined by the **last** class of **recruits**, who return to the College from their eleven month period of service in the forces to start the third and final part of *their* two-year training period. Under the old system, the recruits are, in contrast to the new students, employed and paid by the State. Consequently, they are, from the very beginning of their career as recruits, closely integrated into the hierarchical system of power and control in the police organisation. The first part of their training period covered theoretical and practical training for three months at the College and in special training camps; and the third and final part is a eight month period of theoretical and practical training at the College.

From recruit to student; from two years to three years of basic training: why this change? In various responses to the ongoing reform of police training, both Parliament and the Ministry have focused on the increase, sophistication and internationalisation of crime as an important challenge to police training. But in addition to this traditional perspective on the future role of the police, they have also focused on the general social differentiation of modern society and the need for a more comprehensive understanding of the challenge of new ethnic minorities to policing. Among the possible police responses to this challenge, multi-agency approaches, community policing and migrant and ethnic relations training are mentioned by the Parliament.

The Norwegian context

Norway is an extremely homogeneous society. The challenge of migrants and ethnic minorities to policing is, in quantitative terms, a small one. 3.4 % (roughly 145 000) of the total population (4 millions) are foreigners, and most of them (roughly 92 000) come from Northern Europe and North America.

However, this way of looking at things can be biased. The very fact of cultural homogeneity provides a potential for national chauvinism and racism. A number of racist and violent assaults towards various immigrant groups indicates that Norwegian innocence cannot be taken for granted.

Besides, the perspective of cultural homogeneity may be biased for quite another reason. What tends to look homogeneous from the outside point of view, tends to look pluralistic seen from the inside. The anthropological concept of **cultural variation** could possibly serve as a more promising starting point for police training concerning migrants and ethnic relations. The term "challenge" in the title of this paper is implicitly biased in the sense that it can reinforce the stereotyped view of migrants and ethnic groups as "problem" groups within society. By looking upon ethnicity as one instance of the anthropological concept of cultural variation, this implicit bias could, hopefully, be avoided.

The role of the social sciences in Norwegian police training

The conclusions from the meeting (in 1988) of experts on migrants, ethnic group and the police[1] expressed considerable scepticism towards the approach of police training that amounts "simply to the giving of information on the history, culture and socio-economic situation of different groups of immigrants". On the other hand, the experts also admitted that the task of changing the attitudes of police officers is very difficult and that "some of those involved in such training are indeed shifting the emphasis from trying to change attitudes to making people more aware of their attitudes".

---

[1]   Council of Europe, Addendum to MG-CR (88) 25.

The expert group called for a broader educational approach to police training concerning migrants and ethnic relations. One possible approach along such guidelines is the integration of the social sciences in basic police training. This approach has been adopted by the Norwegian reform[2].

The social science approach of the Norwegian reform covers the following subjects: political science and social anthropology in the first year, criminology in the third and psychology in the first and third year. Altogether, this corresponds to six months of intensive teaching and studying. The rest of the two-year period at the College consists of six months of training in law and court procedures and twelve months of training in the various fields of policing: crime prevention, criminal investigation, law and order maintenance, police tactics, the use of weapons, traffic control, physical training etc.

Among the four subjects mentioned above, the study of social anthropology is no doubt the most relevant study in the context of migrants and ethnic relations. The teaching and study of anthropology is divided in three closely related parts. The first part gives an introduction to the general concepts, theories and perspectives of anthropology, with a special focus on, as already mentioned, the variation of culture. This general and comprehensive perspective is then applied to selected "sub-cultures" of society, among which are the most relevant immigrant and ethnic groups in the Norwegian society. Finally, the anthropological concepts are applied to the occupational culture of the police itself. The intention is to describe the "transactions" between the police and the minorities as "transactions" between different ways of interpreting and constructing social life worlds and to highlight the possibilities and pitfalls inherent in such "transactions".

---

[2]   See also the study by Martin Lightfoot (member of the Home Office Research and Planning Unit) "New Directions in Police training" (1988).

This perspective on training in the area of migrants and ethnic relations draws heavily on an educational scheme developed by the Ministry of Local Government and the Directorate of Immigration. The scheme, which is intended for use in the college system, is part of a more comprehensive scheme of measures against racism and ethnic discrimination in Norway.

As an introduction to the social science training, the students are given an elementary course in statistics and methodology. Although police organisations are important producers of statistical data on crime, they are normally not trained in the use and interpretation of the data they produce. There has been a tendency to jump to conclusions and to disregard the need to interpret even the "hard" facts of social life in terms of a particular problem situation and a particular context of meaning. This is easily seen in the debate on "the race and crime problem". Even if it might be established as a statistical fact that members of immigrant communities commit more crimes of certain types than do members of non-immigrants communities; this fact calls for the use of the well-known explanatory variables of the social sciences: age, gender, social status, income etc. In this sense, then, what looks like inherent characteristics of ethnicity, is reinterpreted in terms of variables that cut across the ethnic variable.

One feature of the twelve-month period of practical service in the local forces needs to be mentioned in this context. The students are supposed to work for a period of eight weeks outside the local police force and take part in the daily activities and routines of a relevant (public or private) institution, agency or organisation: the social services, schools, refugee centres, women crisis centres, hospitals, prisons, anti-drug organisations etc. In this way, the relevance and possibilities of the multi-agency approach to policing should, hopefully, be more easily accepted and appreciated when the students start to work as police officers after finishing their three-year training period. Besides, the eight-week period is intended as a kind of anthropological field work, in the sense that the students are required to write a report on their experiences as participant observers and to describe and interpret the everyday life of the institution or organisation in a systematic way.

The curriculum in social anthropology is partly standard Norwegian text books used in universities and colleges and partly research reports, articles and essays that relate more directly to the questions of particular groups, "cop culture" and ethnicity. Some of the lecturers at the College have a university degree in the social sciences, but in addition, researchers and police officers with a relevant background and experience in the field are asked to lecture. Moreover, representatives of relevant ethnic communities will be invited to attend classes and discuss whatever may be of interest to them and the students. The teaching methods are traditional academic lectures, classroom-teaching, work group session, role play, informal discussion groups, and, of course, self study.

Ethics and human rights

During the first two weeks at the College, the students are given an introductory course in general ethics. This course, developed in collaboration with a professional philosopher (Tore Lindholm) working at the Norwegian Institute of Human Rights in Oslo, is intended to serve as a frame of reference for the teaching in police ethics, which is organised as a separate subject. In general ethics, the focus is on basic ethical concepts, metaethnical theories of the nature of morality and moral arguments and on the three main traditions of moral thinking: teleology, deontology and consequentialism. The principles of general ethics are then applied to cases and dilemmas in police ethics.

Although the intention in general ethics is mainly to develop a more comprehensive understanding of moral reasoning rather than to stress the importance of specific substantial norms and values, the perspective of human rights is introduced in order to show how normative principles designate a crucial part of any valid response to the challenge of multi-ethnic societies. The arguments may be summarized in the following way:

Ethnic conflict is a world-wide phenomenon. On the eve of the 1990's (until Iraq's invasion of Kuwait in August 1990) all of the world's armed conflicts were internal conflicts. At the heart of the conflicts in former

Yugoslavia and the former Soviet Union is the principle of ethno-nationality: each nation, defined in terms of a particular culture, language, religion or life-style, has the right to form its own state and each state ought to contain just one nation. Even if the best response to the violent consequences of ethno-nationalistic aspirations in some cases is to secede from the larger state or empire and establish (or reestablish) an independent nation-state, this does not solve the problems, since the (re)emerging independent state still will have to deal with the unresolved problems of multi-ethnicity.

The challenge of a significant multi-ethnic population is absent only in a tiny minority of all states. The normal state of affairs around the world is that the principle of ethno-nationality is not satisfied and can not be satisfied without a complete redrawal of the present map of state borders; removal of hundreds of millions of people; implementation of forced assimilation programmes; abolition of citizenship; or mass slaughter of all those that stand in the way of the realization of the principle of ethno-nationality.

The emergence of the system of human rights norms, and the international machinery for its implementation, is an amazing triumph of moral and political reasoning, despite the fact of an immense diversity of cultural backgrounds and moral and religious premises. The sovereign states of UN have thus taken on the international duty to safeguard the human rights of every human being under their jurisdiction, at a minimum threshold level, and without any discrimination and exclusion. The means that human rights constitute the moral core of that state power most vital to the ultimate task of maintaining the basic freedoms and the equal dignity of all human beings: the police.

The main reason for including human rights in the curriculum and teaching of general ethics at the Police College is to make clear that the logic behind the ethno-nationalist slogan of Norwegian graffiti - "Norway for Norwegians" - is equivalent to the logic that generates the most threatening and frightful conflicts in the world today. Moreover, the definition of "racism" in the UN convention on the abolition of all forms

107

of racial discrimination serves as a more fruitful starting point for police policy towards ethnic minorities than the often confusing debate on psychological attitudes and individual values.

Specialist training

One of the main objectives of the Norwegian reform is to integrate the Police College in the college and university system and draw upon the resources and knowledge of the well-established academic institutions. However, the plans for advanced training of police officers in the local forces are fragmentary and have not materialized in concrete proposals.

Consequently, advanced training is still given in the form of courses at the College, normally varying from one to nine weeks. In Norway, the police is organized according to the principle of "unitary policing", which implies that the different functions of policing are carried out within the same organisational structure. Because the Norwegian police, on the principle of "unitary policing", have responsibility for immigration control, the particular training needs of those civilians and police officers who work in the aliens departments of local forces, must be met by the College. Since both the former two-year and the present three-year period of basic training include very rudimentary elements of law relevant to immigration control, this need must be met by specialist courses.

Because the two-year system of training included very little of social science/anthropology, the traditional one-week course in alien law and immigration control was replaced by a two-week course in March 1992. In addition to the traditional topics of the one-week course, roughly one of the two weeks was devoted to the following topics:

-    immigration and immigrants: lecture given by an academic of immigrant origin;

-    culture and cultural understanding: police culture and ethnic minorities;

- Iran and Iranian immigrants;

- Islam: a general introduction to the varieties of Islamic culture;

- cross-cultural communication: role play conducted by an anthropologist;

- Turkey and Turkish immigrants.

The course was positively evaluated by the participants, although some of them claimed that alternative lectures on particular ethnic minorities ought to have been included in the course. With the exception of the role play on cross-cultural communication, which was very well received, it seems that a two-week course is too short a period for focus on cultural understanding in general. Future versions of this course will therefore concentrate on the understanding of particular minorities, leaving the general topics of social anthropology for the three-year period of basic training.

Vidar Halvorsen

10. Police College, Solna, Sweden

Introduction

The **Defoir-Project** encompasses proposals for all the stages or levels of training that are carried out at the Police College (PC). Although the proposals of the Defoir-report covered a variety of objectives, curriculum contents and length of courses, the present paper focuses on the programme carried out within basic course 2 (the probationer has to finish basic course 1, which lasts 10 months, and an 18-month period of practice, before starting basic course 2).

Under current proposals, other courses will be the management course for the senior officers (which should start in a totally new shape soon), the Commissioners' courses and a variety of special courses. The latter are to be managed centrally at the PC and they will be specially designed for officers stationed at the borders or otherwise dealing with immigrants and refugees.

Historical background

In 1985 a new training system was introduced for the Swedish police. Among other matters, it concerned the basic training for probationers, which lasts about three years. Three types of objectives, were set out: knowledge, skills/dexterity (a more technical dimension) and attitudes. In 1986 I found that some of the objectives were not covered by the curriculum. It was necessary to remedy these imperfections and deficiencies, which concerned the following elements:

1.   The development of "the understanding of and respect for legal provisions/enactments as a guarantee of *democracy*, justice and legal security/the rule of law".

2. "Knowledge about the *multi-cultural society*" and "the development of understanding of ethnic and other *minorities*".

3. "Deepening understanding as regards the *value of democracy* and enhancement of the ability to identify and scrutinise problems connected with *human rights*, justice and the rule of law".

With the good will of the director of the Police College and of the deputy director of the National Swedish Police Board, we were able to start a curriculum development project named the **Defoir-project**. Its main concern was democracy, human (and humanitarian) rights and inter-ethnic relations.

In this project both the preparatory work by the lecturers and the training itself should take as their starting point laws, legal provisions and similar enactments, e.g. articles in international treaties and conventions. Such an approach carries a methodological advantage, since it is based on the principle that both probationers and serving police officers should loyally apply and enforce existing law. So the Swedish constitution and the international conventions served as basic working tools.

However, although the final report on the project was presented to the Directorate of NSPB in the autumn of 1989 and the reactions were positive, the suggestions in the report have, unfortunately, not yet led to any actual curriculum reforms.

The idea of starting the project was therefore totally independent of any kind of programme of action by the police; it was the result of our perception of the needs resulting from the development of our society.

General remarks

The general or overall model of the course curriculum was designed for all levels of police training and naturally took into account the different needs of the target groups in question. It is founded on constitutional rights and human rights in combination with a code of ethics and conduct. Moreover, this base must permeate all police training. Thus, the main prerequisite for all training and all courses, and in particular for successful multi-cultural or inter-ethnic training, is a preceding thematic course about the above ideals and values. After having passed this gateway, and only then, the probationer or police officer is ready to attend a thematic course on inter-ethnic relations.

Objectives

The **overall instructional objectives** of the syllabus of our model for the field of "Democracy and the multi-cultural society" are as follows:

After the period of study the participant shall have:

- increased his knowledge about and understanding of the nature and conditions of democracy;

- increased his insight into and understanding of the ideals of the Constitution of the country, especially regarding civil rights, the rule of law and personal integrity;

- increased his knowledge about and his understanding of the international community of states, public international law and the rules of the treaties on human rights and of humanitarian laws and measures;

- increased his knowledge about and understanding of the conditions of migration, Swedish culture, other cultures prevalent in Sweden, and the conditions of ethnic groups and of inter-ethnic relations;

- understood the relationship between the ideals and efforts of the international community of states and of the Swedish society concerning human rights, and more fully accepted these ideals;

- on the basis of the above ideals and knowledge, made conclusions concerning his duty on a practical basis and acquired a less rigid and a more tolerant attitude towards the multi-cultural Swedish society;

- increased his knowledge and ability to co-operate with others who strive for the principal aims of society, viz. security, justice and welfare;

- increased his ability to identify, critically analyze and evaluate problems.

We sought to reach these objectives through two one-week courses, the first dealing with the foundation concepts of democracy and human rights and moving on in the second week to the inter-ethnic questions.

Course curriculum - democracy week

The first week was to deal with matters under the following headings: the nature of Swedish democracy (ideals and values), view of man and other general issues, the rule of law, fundamental rights and freedoms, the integrity of the citizen, equal rights and opportunities and domestic provisions against discrimination.

As for topics related to international law and the international community our proposal contained the following topics: the fundamental features of public international law, some relevant parts of international law based on treaties, the Universal UN Declaration and the European Convention on Human Rights and Fundamental Freedoms.

Only one week was allotted to this course and this was far too little for our inter-disciplinary ambitions involving elements of history, religion, ethnography, ethnology and psychology in addition to the more traditional subjects of police sciences and law.

Course curriculum - multi-cultural week -

The thematic week on "The multi-cultural society" was designed and carried out from the autumn of 1988 until the summer of 1990. Almost 400 probationers (from basic course 2) underwent this training. As a compromise, some important elements of the former week were in fact carried out during the multicultural week.

Day 1: Constitutional and human rights day. A member of the UNHCR staff gave a lecture on human rights.

Day 2: Concepts like ethnicity and other scientific terms and "Swedishness" would be dealt with. A lecturer with an immigrant background would give his personal view on the "dilemma of exile".

Day 3: One representative of either the old minorities, or preferably of the newly-arrived groups, would give information and discuss background factors, cultural elements of his/her group and the situation of the group in Swedish society. An "internal" discussion followed the course.

Day 4: This was the day of religion and cultural encounters. Professors of religious science or outside experts dealt with these matters.

Day 5: Outside experts dealt with matters like ethnic discrimination and the legal provisions against it, as well as racist organisations in Sweden. A part of this day was used to evaluate this thematic week. This day was bound to bring in quite specifically the issues of racist and xenophobic behaviour.

Methodology

A high degree of activity among the participants was one of the most important **methodological** ends. This was of course due to the fact that the objectives took attitudes into account. The free discussion among classmates had great value itself, whatever the size of the group. There was team work in small groups and discussions in the class as a whole (including us, the two facilitators).

Staffing

Most of our trainers were civilians with an academic background. But no matter what background a trainer has, it is essential that he/she in turn undergoes a continuous training process. When inviting external or internal experts, one aimed of course, to choose the real experts. The probationers were very critical and so we had to aim to get the best possible trainers.

The permanent staff, also need to be engaged in a continuous learning process (visits to police and other institutions abroad, attending seminars, courses, conferences and colloquies in Sweden and abroad).

The series of nordic seminars

In addition to the project itself a series of seminars were hold in 1989-1990 in co-operation with the Finnish and Norwegian police training institutions (Denmark participated as a corresponding party). The Finnish Ministry of the Interior and the Norwegian Ministry of Justice supported the seminars in a most positive way[1,2].

---

1 Report: «A Nordic Experience of Developing New Ideas in the Field of Human Rights, Constitutional Rights and Ethics» (DH-ED-COLL (90) 12), Council of Europe.

2 «Aspects on Policing/Police Training and Human Rights. — General issues and recent development in Sweden» prepared by T. Soukkan (DH-ED-COLL (90) 13), Council of Europe.

116

Evaluation

By 1989 and 1990 more than 90 % of our students were in favour of the course as described. This was a considerable improvement compared to the autumn of 1988, when about 75 % of the participants gave the course a similar mark.

Lessons learnt/difficulties encountered

a.   Not more than two experts per day should be brought in if the discussion are to be fruitful.

b.   Some probationers had negative attitudes to the topic itself which of course created a difficult atmosphere. That is why the facilitators should always be at least two in number.

c.   It is enormously difficult to make such abstract parts of the course as constitutional and human rights seem concrete and a more multi-disciplinary approach would help.

d.   The lecturers at the PC are of course supposed to assess not only the knowledge but also the skills and the attitudes of the probationer. It is very difficult to find an appropriate balance between, on the one hand, fostering an open and free discussion in the class and, on the other hand, measuring an individual's racist or xenophobic inclination.

In conclusion, I will try to list some of the crucial elements of the **Defoir-programme**:

-       The period of study should be based on a positive anthropology (in the sense of view of man/the individual/the citizen).

-       The participants should be offered a real opportunity for individual development throughout the period of study.

- The period of study should be permeated by a multi-disciplinary approach taking into account the process of internationalisation.

- The multi-disciplinary approach must secure the highest degree of integration of various relevant subjects of the curriculum.

- The best structural and methodological design would be a thematic period on inter-ethnic issues.

- Such a thematic period should precede all other subjects at every level of training (all officers need the training).

- Teaching of the different subjects should later involve elements of inter-ethnic issues when naturally needed.

- The constitutional and human rights constitute a part of the important infrastructure for the inter-ethnic training and, indeed, for all police training.

Türker Soukkan

11. Police Staff College Bramshill, United Kingdom

The "police and ethnic minorities course"
at the Police Staff College, Bramshill, U.K.

History

The subject of race relations was part of the academic curriculum at Bramshill throughout the 1960s and all the command courses had significant community relations modules.

In 1982 it was decided to introduce a range of short courses, most often of one or two weeks' duration, catering for special training needs. The "*Police and Ethnic Minorities*" course was in the original list of short courses (then known as "carousel" courses) and was directed at operational officers commanding divisions and sub-divisions in areas of ethnic minority concentration.

In 1992, after a course review involving consultation with the Director of the Specialist Support Unit for Police Community and Race Relations Training at Turvey, Bedfordshire, the course was renamed "*Police and Visible Minorities*", slightly playing down the emphasis on culture and ethnicity and enhancing the emphasis on colour and other physical traits acting as indicators of minority social status. This has enabled women and disabled people to be given consideration on the course, though the bulk of the time is still given to people with South Asian and Afro-Caribbean backgrounds.

Policy context

More recently, the policy emphasis has shifted in two directions, both highly complementary to police community and race relations.

The first is **"Equal Opportunities"**, and concerns the fairness of employment practices within the organisation rather than relations with members of the public.

The second is **"Quality of Service"**, which concerns meeting the requirements of the public, who are seen as the "customer" of the police service, and also meeting the needs of departments and divisions within the organisation, as a necessary prelude to providing adequate public service.

At the Police Staff College, short courses on Equal Opportunities for force personnel officers were introduced in 1990 and on Quality of Service in Policing in 1991. The latter course is attended both by headquarters officers responsible for force inspection, complaints and discipline, management services etc. and by operational officers with command responsibilities.

The **"Police and Visible Minorities"** *course is the only one of those mentioned to focus on ethnic minority groups.*

On the longer "*Command Courses*", it is usual for a day or more to be specifically dedicated to each of the above-mentioned topics, but it is also intended that awareness of the relevance of issues of quality, equality, community, ethnicity etc. should permeate the course and not be confined to those occasions when the subjects are directly addressed.

Training at the Staff College is the peak of a national system of training, which takes place at District Training Centres around the country and also in force. A Police Training Council report on training in community and race relations of 1983 set out a comprehensive curriculum covering all ranks up to Assistant Chief Constable. Resource problems have been substantial, but particularly since the establishment of the Specialist Support Unit for Community and Race Relations Training under the experienced Directorship of Jerome Mack, a black American who had done similar work for the U.S. armed services for many years before developing a private consultancy specialism in Britain, real progress has been made and a coordinated approach to training in this area is gathering momentum.

The Home Office has been instrumental in this progress, but greater commitment and cooperation amongst the police staff associations, particularly the Association of Chief Police Officers and the Police Federation (representing ranks from constable to chief inspector) have also been significant factors.

Objectives

The course has two general objectives:

-       to enhance understanding of visible minorities' experience and perceptions, together with relevant aspects of minority cultures, and

-       to enhance the quality of policing provided to members of visible minorities, both in the context of service delivery and law enforcement, and also within the organisation as well as in relations with the public.

The specific objectives are for the officers at the end of the course to be more effective and efficient in:

(a)   policing areas of ethnic minority concentration, with a view to ensuring that the same quality of service is provided as in other areas;

(b)   responding appropriately to national community/race relations/equal opportunities policies, with a view to ensuring that the best standards and practices are widely disseminated;

(c)   understanding the experience and perspectives of the visible minorities and assessing their policing needs, with a view to ensuring that the quality of policing received by visible minorities is based on sound and sensitive awareness of the groups concerned;

(d)   drawing on minority groups as sources of support and police personnel, with a view to ensuring that minority people are not perceived, *ipso facto*, as "problems", whether criminal or otherwise;

(e)   devising and implementing a policing strategy which will provide quality police services to visible minorities, with a view to ensuring that there are no "second class citizens" in the policing context.

Course curriculum

From its inception, the course has been two weeks in duration, but this year a second part of a day and a half has been added to allow members to undertake a project in the six months between the two parts. This second part strengthens the practicality of the course, assists dissemination of practical knowledge based on the experience of the members of the course in applying what they have learned, and also assists course evaluation.

The course gives detailed attention to the need to understand and respect immigrant cultures and also focuses on the problem of racist violence. The latter issue has been of major concern to the Home Office and to several police forces for over a decade and has given rise to a succession of official reports and police responses.

Methods and materials

The course is designed to give its members ample opportunity to learn from each other; to question policy-makers and specialists in the subject; and to develop their own plans to tackle the problems relevant to them and their particular responsibilities.

The one day force visit is valuable in providing an opportunity to discuss police community relations matters whilst the perspectives developed on the course are fresh in mind.

The materials provided for the course are as follows:

- a course handbook setting out the course rationale and the objectives for each session, together with question prompts;

- a course reader providing short articles relevant to the seminars and exercises;

- a bound set of Home Office and other official reports or extracts on the subject;

- various seminar and exercise papers;

- papers distributed by visiting speakers.

Participants

The course was designed for local commanders and their deputies. Initially, those working in areas of ethnic minority concentration were deemed to be most in need of the course, but it is now considered that commanders in all areas must be catered for, especially as the curriculum has widened to include other vulnerable groups.

Staffing

The Course Tutor is responsible for the design and running of the course as a whole, and for acting as facilitator in a number of training sessions, particularly those concerned with the concepts and theories which underpin the rationale of the course, and with the sociological and psychological aspects of the syllabus.

The Course Tutor is a sociologist with many years experience of higher police training. In the last two years he has attended the six week course for community and race relations/equal opportunities trainers at the Specialist Support Unit for community and Race Relations Training referred to above, and has also attended staff training workshops conducted by external consultants at the Staff College. In addition to his academic training at university, he has received both teacher training and training in the methodology and skills of group facilitation.

Visiting speakers to the course include senior police officers, members of the Home Office and Her Majesty's Inspectorate of Constabulary, ethnic minority officers, members of the Directing staff and outside academics/trainers and consultants. Minority group persons conducting session include black people, women and a disabled person.

Evaluation

Course critique forms are completed by each course member and these are considered when planning each course.

The introduction of a two-stage structure, with a six month period in between for project work in force has not only significantly enhanced the effectiveness of the course but has enabled a much more confident assessment of impact to be achieved.

In conclusion it may be said that, whilst the course does not attempt the dubious undertaking of addressing deep-seated emotional attitudes and culturally-determined presuppositions (i.e. the course rejects the radical methodology of "Racism Awareness Training" in which the individual's own racism and race guilt are confronted head on) awareness of issues is significantly raised and, more importantly, commitment to address problems in the right spirit and with the appropriate practical skills is genuinely enhanced.

Norman Greenhill

12. Initiatives taken
in England and Wales

The police service in England and Wales is comprised of 43 different forces. We are not a national police service and a national police inspectorate has the duty to assess the efficiency of forces and to ensure they work broadly within policy guidelines.

The previous thirty years service have seen most of the important changes in the way we deliver policing services to communities of minority ethnic origin. In England and Wales we have had a multi-cultural society since the end of the second world war, but perhaps we lacked foresight, persistence, commitment and most of all a coherent long term strategy to bring about change.

We have had training strategies, some well thought out involving representatives of the ethnic minority communities, often led by dedicated trainers. We have had policing strategies as well, the introduction of specialist community liaison officers in London in the 1960s followed by the rest of the country in the early 1970s. We have had policies, government policy in particular, though seldom accompanied by resources. Policies concerned with recruiting officers from ethnic minority communities. We had good advice from many sources, including ethnic minority communities and their representatives, government and government agencies and not least from academic researchers. We have had goodwill; police have not created the tensions of a multi-racial society, but nevertheless they have failed until recently to learn how to deal with them.

Why then did our training initiatives fail to bring about the desired results until recently? It was because, like many identified problems which require major change as part of the solution, training and training alone was given the responsibility of bringing about that change. So what can be done to ensure that the training currently being done succeeds and brings about the desired result?

First we decide what we want to achieve. Police officers want to have the knowledge and the confidence to deliver a policing service to the public where members of the public have differing origins such; knowledge needs to encompass the plural nature of our society. Confidence has to be based on professional policing knowledge relative to needs of the community. Lack of confidence and knowledge on the part of police officers leads to lack of performance. That lack of performance is interpreted by those communities as indifference or hostility leading to lack of confidence in the police. Lack of confidence in the police makes their task more difficult and so the damaging spiral leads to a breakdown of communication and lack of contact.

So training must have the aim of making police officers more successful. What is required from police officers must be stated clearly in order that training is related to those professional requirements and is a positive benefit rather than a negative corrective. We must know and clearly state what we wish training to achieve and we must have objective criteria to assess its results.

In the United Kingdom one example of the way this has been achieved is by having a strong policy statement on how the police respond to racially motivated attacks. This statement endorsed by all Chief Officers is reinforced by a parliamentary scrutiny of the subject from time to time. The Home Office circulate guidance on how to achieve success in policing racial attacks and the Inspectorate rigorously examine the performance of forces in relation to their response to victims and success in identifying offenders. In addition the Home Office sponsored the development of a national training package by the police in cooperation with a university.

The elements for a successful training initiative were therefore assembled. A clear statement of policy. The provision of training resources for trainers to train in support of the policy. An evaluation of the success of the training in bringing about a more effective police response to the problem of racially motivated attacks. The message to the police officer is clear, in order to be a successful police officer you must be able to deal effectively with this policing problem. Not failure, not blame, not criticism unless professional standards are not met.

If the United Kingdom now has a reasonably comprehensive range of training initiatives, which taken together are beginning to have an effect on police officers and policing methods, it came into being not as a grand strategy but as a series of initiatives each of which exposed a weakness or weaknesses which prevented a successful outcome. Perhaps, therefore, they were successful by exposing those limitations and the need to do more. But that was not their aim. The aims of early initiatives were usually to train police officers in dealing with communities which were seen as "difficult". The training was perceived to concentrate on difficulties and the attendant risks of failure and there was little incentive to volunteer for such training or to see that it was central to being a successful police officer.

The training initiative which has existed for longer than any other, now twenty five years, is, significantly, aimed at the senior ranks of the service. A week long seminar, known as the *Holly Royde Seminar*, is held each year at Manchester University and senior officers from many forces bring to the seminar an identified policing issue centred on community and race relations which they examine during the course of the week and develop action plans they will be responsible for implementing over the following year. This seminar is noted for the quality of the contributors. Ministers of the Crown, the senior civil servant in charge of the Home Office, her Majesty's Chief Inspector of Constabulary, Jerome Mack and the Commissioner of the Metropolitan Police to name but a distinguished few. The course is run by an academic director who is leader in this field and the facilities are first class.

The Inspectorate also plays a part in the Seminar. The implementation of the action plans developed by senior officers will be examined during the course of the following year. The seminar is held in January, and during September the participants are required to prepare a progress report and these are examined and many will receive a visit from the Inspectorate. If they are successful they may well be invited back to tell the next year's seminar how that success was achieved.

Those elements so essential for the success of a training initiative are present in abundance in this seminar which may account for its longevity. There is clear statement of the aim of the training reinforced by the commitment of those senior figures who contribute to the seminar. Resources are available to ensure the training is effective and to reinforce the commitment to success. Lastly there is an evaluation, a longer term assessment of the success of participants which again emphasizes the aim of the training in support of the policy aims.

Training senior officers can be a frustrating business. They are ambitious and in demand. They move frequently, too frequently in the judgement of some, and so often the immediate benefits of that training are not communicated downward to police officers working under their command.

It was the policy of dedicating some police officers to specialist work as Community Liaison Officers in the late 60s and early 70s which identified the need for a specific training initiative aimed at making them more knowledgeable, more professional and more confident in their new role. A school with good facilities, was contracted to run the training. The Home Office reinforced the aims of the training by officially inviting forces to send participants and ensuring all Chief Officers were aware of the course and its objectives. Again the importance of the course is demonstrated by the contributors who include not just senior police officers but members of many other agencies and communities. The Inspectorate requires forces to give details of the amount of training in community and race relations undertaken each year. This course has now been running over ten years and has been reviewed and adjusted to meet changes in the role as necessary. Aims, resources and evaluation, each of the elements necessary for success are present.

The major initiative on community and race relations training had the worst of beginnings. It stemmed from the report of Lord Justice Scarman who investigated the major public disorders which recurred in 1981. Those disorders clearly indicated a lack of knowledge on the part of the police of the conditions existing in ethnic minority communities and a lack of police professionalism in dealing with those communities.

128

To be fair, other agencies were also identified as lacking knowledge and professionalism but it was the police on whom those communities had concentrated their frustration and bitterness born of lack of confidence in the police. The Scarman report recommended greater training for the police, and the Police Training Council, a Home office committee, published their working party report which proposed a strategy for community and race relations training.

Central to that strategy was the creation of an independent unit supporting police efforts in community and race relations training. That independent unit is now the *Specialist Support Unit* headed by Jerome Mack. It has clearly defined and stated policy objectives. They are regularly restated by the Home Office in their sponsoring of the courses for police trainers. They are formed and periodically examined by the management board of the unit which includes representative of Chief Officers and the representatives of police officers at all levels of the service.

The resources given to the *Specialist Support Unit* to sustain a five year strategy to achieve its aim is an indication of the commitment of the government to its success. Police forces respond by sending their trainers to be trained in community and race relations issues in order that they can return to their forces to train all officers in these issues. The unit employs leading professionals in the field of community and race relations in addition to police liaison officers who perform duty at the unit.

The evaluation is carried out by the Inspectorate. A report by the Inspectorate helped to identify a revised set of aims for the next two years.

One major finding of that evaluation was that trainers cannot bring about change without the support of the top management of the force. It is essential to require the senior management to state their policy aims so that they may make effective use of their most valuable resource, the newly skilled trainers produced by the *Specialist Support Unit*.

Another major finding of the evaluation was that although the Specialist Support Unit was established to support police training in community and race relations the two major police training bodies (The Central Planning and Training Unit which deals with training of officers from the start of their service to the middle ranks and the Police Staff college which deals with the training of officers of more senior rank) were not developing with the Specialist Support unit the necessary strategies to ensure effective training in community and race relations throughout an officer's career. This omission devalues the efforts of the Specialist Support Unit which may be seen to lie outside the main training effort of the service. The Police Staff College and Central Planning and Training Unit are therefore not aware of and can not share in the expertise of the unit in developing police training strategies. New aims have been drawn up for the Specialist Support Unit to ensure that these areas are addressed. The policies of the Central Planning and Training Unit and the Police Staff College include a clear statement of policy, followed by the commitment of resources and a dedication to evaluate the effectiveness of their work.

It is only by constantly evaluating the effect of the training process that the necessary changes and additions to the overall strategy can be identified and implemented. A constant examination of police performance in these areas and a rigorous examination of the results achieved by training are necessary to identify new areas which need to be addressed.

Equally policy makers cannot identify strategies and then handover the total responsibility to the trainers. They must ensure that resources are committed and they must also ensure that the end result is what was intended and any obstacles to the training are overcome. Where lack of supporting initiatives are identified as preventing the training being effective then new initiatives must be put in place in order to overcome this.

Because the training in community and race relations is now seen by officers to affect their professional training at each stage of their service, the importance of that training is enhanced and the training is not seen as a special training.

It has always been clear that confidence in the police by ethnic minority communities cannot be better demonstrated than by their willingness to become part of the Police Service. The first officers of ethnic minority origin joined the service over 25 years ago but they remained few in number and marginal in that they were seen as "black police officers" or "Asian police officers" rather than "police officers". More recently a clear policy of encouraging the recruitment of ethnic minority officers has been stated by the Home Office reinforced by parliamentary scrutiny and endorsed by chief officers. Extra resources in order to encourage forces with large ethnic minority communities to recruit from those communities have been provided by the Home office and encouragement has been provided by the Home office and encouragement has been given by the Inspectorate through examining the efforts of all forces in relation to this recruiting initiative. Progress over the first 20 years was painfully slow. It is now slightly less slow. In the past five years we have increased the number of police officers of ethnic minority origin both men and women from a total of just over 1,000 to 1,659. This still only represents 1.3 % of the Police Service but the success of the policy is becoming increasingly evident.

Wherever I have spoken to officers about the benefits of having ethnic minority officers in the service they have been very positive. The benefit does not come from those officers policing their own communities but by being part of the service passing on their knowledge and skills to make all police officers more capable and more professional in policing those communities. It reinforces the training message. I am well aware that the status of people of ethnic minority origin in some of the countries represented here is not the same as in the United Kingdom. Nonetheless the delivery of a good policing service which addresses the needs of the individual not based on the colour of their skin or their status as citizens is the fundamental message of any successful training in community and race relations. After 31 years of service I have seen a tremendous change in the way officers treat people of ethnic minority origin. Because of their increased knowledge and because of their confidence in their professional ability to deliver an appropriate service they do not see themselves dealing with "difficult" customers or "different" clients. They deal with members of the public who have the right to expect a non discriminatory police service delivered by well trained professional police officers.

This aim can only be said to have been achieved when we can present evidence to demonstrate it is the normal outcome of policing activity. Increasingly in the United Kingdom police performance will be monitored to ensure that it is delivered fairly and non discriminatorily. Key activities such as the stopping and searching of citizens, the arrest and detention of citizens, and the way that prisoners are dealt with will be monitored to ensure that service delivery by the police is based on equal opportunities. The Inspectorate will play its part in requiring information on which these judgements can be based. If our training initiatives have been successful given the resources and efforts devoted to them then this will be their most significant and may I suggest their final and most appropriate evaluation.

J.D. Moore
HM Inspectorate of Constabulary

13. Specialist Support Unit, United Kingdom

Historical background

Beginning in the late 1940's, settlement by migrants from Britain's erstwhile colonies in Asia, Africa and the Caribbean has transformed Britain into a multi-racial, multi-cultural society. This has placed new demands on public-service agencies, which have been used to operating in a virtually mono-ethnic environment. In the case of the police, there have also been tensions in relationships with the visible minority communities, especially with young black and Asian people who have grown up in Britain.

The riots in London and other British cities in 1981 disturbed any complacency. Lord Scarman's report on *The Brixton Disorders* proposed major changes in police training. The Police Training Council (PTC), a national advisory body, produced a report entitled *Community and Race Relations Training for the Police*, which set out a whole series of recommendations designed to ensure that these issues should become an integral part of all police training. The PTC report set out a series of principles and stressed that *all* officers should receive such training throughout their careers. The authors drew up a set of principles and emphasised that all police officers should receive their training throughout their career.

The first^U independent training support centre did not win the confidence and cooperation of the police service generally, and had little significant impact on police training at the national level; its original five-year contract was not therefore renewed. The government's view, however, was that the general recommendations of the 1983 PTC report were still relevant, and the Home Office decided to establish a "Specialist Support Centre"

Current policy context

Several important developments at national policy level have provided a supportive environment for the work of the new Unit:

1.   A Home Office Circular required all police forces to adopt policies on equal opportunities in employment (though not yet in relation to service delivery).

2.   Legal actions brought against the police by minority officers and members of the public (notably the successful case of P.C.Singh v. Nottinghamshire Constabulary) have increased the pressure for an effective policy response.

3.   The Association of Chief Police Officers has recently produced a strong policy statement which deals with the service delivery aspect of policing (ACPO Strategic Policy Document 1990). The document stresses the importance of meeting community expectations in the delivery of police services, and of ensuring fairness and a high standard of quality in this respect.

4.   The Home Office has produced comprehensive guidance to police and other agencies for dealing with racial attacks (Racial Attacks Group Reports 1989, 1991), and a requirement has been included in the recent Criminal Justice Act 1991 that service delivery by police and other criminal justice agencies be subject to ethnic monitoring.

New "Specialist Support Unit"

The new **"Specialist Support Unit"** (SSU) was established at the Equalities Associates' residential training centre at Turvey in Bedfordshire in 1989. The Director of Equalities Associates and also of the new Unit is Mr Jerome Mack, who was previously a chief of police and a staff member of the Defense Equal Opportunity Management Institute (DEOMI) in the USA. The work of the Unit is supervised by a Management Board which consists mainly of representatives of the Home Office and senior police management.

The SSU's brief requires it to work with more than fifty training establishments. To accomplish its objectives on this scale, the SSU has adopted a strategic approach to its task. The three main elements of this strategy have been: (a) to create a cadre of police trainers nationally who have specialist skills; (b) to design training programmes (and support materials) for these trainers to deliver in their own training establishments; and (c) to undertake strategic planning with the management of those establishments to ensure implementation of these programmes and the integration of community and race relations into wider training curriculum. Particular importance has been attached to the involvement of members of minority communities in the Unit's work.

Objectives

Broadly speaking, the overall function of the Specialist Support Unit remains that set out by the Police Training Council in 1983, i.e. to assist the British police service to develop the community and race relations aspect of police training. The 1983 report continues to provide the basis of current thinking about the way forward in this area.

The specific objectives of the new Unit were defined as follows:

a.   to provide advice and assistance in the development of community and race relations strategies as an integral part of police training strategies nationally;

b.   to train police trainers at national, regional and force level in community and race relations issues;

c.   to establish a community and race relations training resource bank;

d.   to facilitate input to police training from lay contributors;

e. to provide advice and assistance to individual police forces on the content and delivery of the community and race relations element of their training programmes;

f. to disseminate relevant information and research.

Staffing

The Unit has a core *staff* of eight, which is multi-racial in composition and includes two police officers on secondment. One of the police officers is responsible for police liaison at a management level, while the main responsibility of the other is to work jointly with civilian staff in delivering training at the classroom level. The civilian staff bring a wide range of experience and expertise from the fields of training and of community and race relations. One of the civilian staff holds particular responsibility for liaison with community groups and for securing community participation in the SSU's programme.

Programme of work

In its most simplified form, this programme has consisted of three components, which in combination form the basic strategy of the SSU: the provision of a specialist *six-week trainers course*, to equip trainers to deliver a *four-phase training programme*, for implementation throughout the police service by means of *strategic planning*. The three components may be summarised as follows:

i. *The Six-Week Trainers Course.* The aim of this course is to produce a cadre of trainers with specialist knowledge and skills, capable of development work and distributed across police training establishments nationally. To establish this course successfully was the initial priority of the Unit, so as to create confidence within the police service, and also within the minority communities who contribute to the course in a variety of ways.

ii.   *The Four-Phase Training Programme.* This training programme is designed to be implemented in all police forces throughout the country. The first three phases consist of training packages to be delivered direct to all officers by graduates of the six-week course, with support from the staff of the SSU. The fourth phase provides for integration of community and race relations issues in mainstream training.

iii.   *Strategic Planning.* This is undertaken with individual police forces and other training establishments. The aim is to enable them to gain full benefit from the services provided by the Unit, and to integrate community and race relations effectively within their training and organisational systems. A two-week *Training Managers Course* is being introduced to assist with strategic planning work.

In order to support these major components, the Unit's programme of work has also included the creation of a *Resource Bank* of relevant community and race relations training materials, and the production of a quarterly *Newsletter* which is distributed widely within the police service. An international edition covered developments in several European countries and also in Australia, Canada and the USA.

Six-week trainers course

The broad aim of the six-week course is to equip trainers with the knowledge, skills and confidence to deal with community and race relations issues in both the design and delivery of training within their own training establishments. It is intended that graduates of the course return to act as change agents within their organisation.

-       *Participants*

The course has been designed specifically for police trainers, and assumes that they have already proficient in basic training skills. Attendance is not a result of personal application but of nomination by the management of the training school. Participants are expected to be briefed as to the tasks they are to undertake subsequently, and to receive management support after their return. Almost all participants are of Sergeant or Inspector rank.

- *Curriculum design*

The curriculum of the six-week course is constructed on a "building-block" model. Each Block builds upon the knowledge and skills that have been acquired before. The Block structure in use throughout the first three years is as follows:

- socialisation and orientation;

- individual and group behaviour with particular reference to cross-cultural communication;

- cross-cultural knowledge in the context of an examination of inter-group relations and minority responses to dominance generally;

- aspects of discrimination, "indirect" ways of discrimination;

- police-community relations (including racial attacks);

- developing CRR training;

- practicum;

- re-entry.

- *Training methods and materials*

Each Block, and each of the lessons within it, is designed to attain specific learning objectives, at both cognitive and affective levels. A wide variety of training methods are employed, with the main emphasis being on student-centred and experiential learning activities. Group exercises and discussions predominate, supported by lecture and video presentations as appropriate. Graduates are also encouraged to generate their own locally relevant training materials, and this has been done with great success in some cases.

- *Community involvement*

Members of minority communities act as external contributors to the course on a regular basis and in a number of different roles, providing expertise not covered by Unit staff, and sharing experience on a personal basis with students. The high level of community involvement in the course is an important element in SSU strategy and is intended to demonstrate good practice to students to be followed in their own training establishments. Community involvement sensitises police officers to community perceptions and expectations.

- *Host-family interface*

The most important interface session included within the course is the "host-family interface", in which each participant spends the third weekend of the course as a guest in a visible minority household. This is invariably a powerful learning experience for the students, many of whom have had little if any close personal contact with black or minority ethnic families. These placements are arranged through local Racial Equality Councils or through ethnic or religious associations. Careful planning and briefing of all those involved is essential. The placements have been arranged in variety of towns and cities, including Leicester, Liverpool and London.

- *Evaluation and review*

Monitoring and evaluation are continuous processes throughout each course, with responses being gathered daily, for each Block and for the course as a whole. In addition a six-month follow-up survey is conducted to obtain a retrospective validation of the course, and an assessment of its impact on the graduate's subsequent work. While these exercises have consistently produced very positive assessments of the course in general terms, two specific concerns have been recurrently expressed by participants:

- the main concern of students while participating in the course has been the lack of time and flexibility to address certain issues in depth, especially where there is sensitivity and strong feelings are involved. Six weeks may seem a long while, but there is strong time pressure resulting from the fact that the curriculum has been condensed from a *sixteen*-week original in the USA. It is also relevant that British police training has recently shifted radically in style from a tightly-programmed didactic mode to a flexible student-centred approach in which trainers focus on affect and skill.

- the second main concern, expressed by those who have graduated from the course, is that they felt they were not sufficiently prepared for the resistance to change they would meet, and not adequately skilled to handle it.

As a result of these concerns, and from recommendations arising from the official evaluation of the Unit, the curriculum described above has been reviewed, and a revised version has been introduced on a pilot basis. Some non-essential curriculum content has been cut out, and skills-based "assessment centres" introduced in the early Blocks. Also, the original Blocks F, G and H have been combined to form a single new Block F, entitled "The Way Forward". This aims to prepare participants more effectively for their role as change agents in a strategic process, with special emphasis on negotiating skills and tackling resistance to change.

Four-phase training programme

the six-week course creates a cadre of trainers capable of delivering community and race relations training to their fellow- officers. The Four-Phase Training Programme is the vehicle by means of which the graduates deliver such training nationwide.

The Four-phase programme (which once again is designed on a building-block model) consists of three phases which are delivered as specialist inputs direct to all police officers in each force over a short period of time, and a final phase in which community and race relations issues are integrated into ongoing mainstream training. It thus combines an initial "blanketing" of all serving police officers with an insertion of the issues into existing training to meet all future needs.

The four phases are as follows:

Phase I: **Awareness**

This phase concentrates on awareness-raising, and has three main aims: to generate firstly an understanding and self-awareness of prejudice and discrimination (both personal and institutional), secondly an appreciation of the harm these can do to the police service, and thirdly personal and organisational strategies for eliminating them.

Phase II: **Knowledge**

This phase increases the knowledge-base on legislation, and on cultural and other factors affecting police-community relations and minority officers within the police. A handbook with ten case exercises and extensive supporting material provides the basis for this phase of the programme.

Phase III: **Skills**

This phase will focus on providing the practical skills necessary for interacting with members of minority ethnic communities. An interactive video and associated workbook will be produced in support.

Phase IV: **Follow on programme**

This phase aims for community and race relations issues to become "threaded" throughout the generic police training curriculum, thus providing for a continuing effect that will support the immediate impact of the three phases above.

The delivery of the first three phases is being conducted by graduates of the six-week course for all ranks up to Chief Inspector, while workshops for Superintendents and above in each force are conducted by staff of the SSU. The delivery of a one-day programme force-wide will in most forces occupy one or two trainers between three and nine months full-time (depending on the size of the force).

To allocate resources on this scale (including staff withdrawal time) requires a genuine commitment to the issues on the part of senior management.

Strategic planning

From the outset, the Unit sought to adopt a strategic approach to its work, seeking through visits and consultations to secure top-down support from senior officers and training managers for the participation of trainers in the six-week course. Trainers attend the course as nominees of their organisation: it is expected that they would be briefed as to why they are being sent, the work they would undertake subsequently, and confident in having management support.

While some students have found themselves well provided for in this way, the Unit's evaluation programme has consistently shown that a substantial minority of students do not feel they receive adequate organisational support. While some have been able to use their new skills and knowledge to play important developmental roles in their organisation, others have not been given such opportunities or have been allowed only limited scope. To overcome this difficulty, and to enhance the effectiveness of the Unit's work across the police training system nationally, a programme is being introduced for strategic planning to be undertaken with each individual training establishment. Such plans are intended to ensure that participation by trainers in the six- week course, and subsequently delivery of the four-phase training programme, both form part of a strategic programme of developmental work which is appropriately resourced and supported by management at all levels.

To service the formulation and implementation of such strategic plans, the Unit will introduce a new two-week **"Training Managers Course"**. This will be designed to increase managers' awareness and understanding of community and race relations issues, and to provide practical assistance with the formulation of strategy and specific action plans. Participation in this training managers course will in turn be preceded by seminars conducted with senior officers from each force, which will be designed to establish a firm policy commitment for the training development work to be undertaken in each organisation.

As a result of this strengthening of the strategic element in the Unit's programme of work, it is now envisaged that developmental work in all training establishments will progress through *six stages*:

1.   *Establishment of organisational commitment*, at senior officer level, with the aid of policy-oriented seminars.

2.   *Formulation of development strategy*, undertaken by training managers, with the aid of the Training Managers Course.

3.   *Train officers for development tasks*, through participation of selected trainers in the Six-Week Course.

4.   *Development of training staff*, undertaken by graduates of the Six-Week Course, who transfer learning and skills to colleagues.

5.   *Develop and implement curricula*, in which graduates lead the delivery of specialist training force-wide, and integrate issues into existing curricula - according to the Four-Phase Programme.

6.   *Evaluation and review*, conducted by management to assess the effectiveness of the programme, and make changes as required.

It should be stressed that a number of police forces have already made substantial progress in moving through these stages. The aims of the SSU's strategy are to bring all forces into the net, to promote effectiveness, and to encourage national consistency.

The future

In the long run, however, it is not work with local police forces that is most important, but with the establishments responsible for training at the national level. A crucial component of the Unit's work during its remaining two years will therefore involve developing closer cooperation with the Police Staff College at Bramshill (PSC) and the Central Planning and Training Unit at Harrogate (CPTU). These are responsible for the more senior and junior levels of national police training respectively.

Work is already progressing in both these training establishments to integrate community and race relations issues into established training curricula. The SSU contributes to both the design and delivery of these aspects of training at the PSC and the CPTU in a variety of ways. In both organisations, graduates of the Six-Week Course are working with colleagues to formulate and implement strategic development plans for this aspect of training.

The SSU will work particularly closely with the *Police Staff College* in carrying out the "strategic planning" component of its programme of work, in view of the PSC's responsibility for middle and senior management training. This will involve cooperation in the design and delivery of the new Training Managers Course and the seminars for senior officers which will precede it. The SSU will be assisted in this task by the long experience of the PSC in running a specialist course on these issues.

Close cooperation with the **Central Planning and Training Unit** is also crucial, since the CPTU is in many ways the motor of the police training system generally. Not only does it design training for Constable, Sergeant and Inspector ranks, but it also trains the trainers who will deliver such training at force or regional levels, as well as monitoring its delivery and evaluating its effectiveness. Since the CPTU is strongly committed to a student-centred approach to training, and to including community and race relations as an integral "theme", the effectiveness with which these issues are dealt with will depend strongly on the commitment and skills of individual trainers. Over the next two years the SSU will work closely with the CPTU on trainer and curriculum development, since in the long run it is only by this means that community and race relations issues will become an integral and enduring component of the British police training system.

Robin Oakley and Jerome Mack

II. Results of
the questionnaire survey

1.   Background

The decades since the end of the Second World War have seen unprecedented levels of immigration into European nations. States which have mostly been born of nationalist movements, and many of which have seen themselves as countries of "emigration", now possess significant minorities within their resident population who are of migrant origin and of different cultural and ethnic identity.

One major strand of this movement has been the migration from countries of southern Europe to those of the north. A second has been the economic migration into Europe from countries of the Third World, in many cases colonial or former colonial territories of European nations. A third and predominantly recent development has been the movement of refugees from many parts of the world into countries in the European domain. These movements have often resulted in tensions between indigenous and migrant groups, characterised in extreme cases by racial and xenophobic violence. In a number of countries these tensions have also extended to relations between groups of migrant origin and the police.

All European nations have been affected to some degree: some earlier and on a more substantial scale, and others only recently and so far to a small extent. However, given the general economic and political pressures towards migration in the modern world, this development may be expected to continue for the foreseeable future. Given also the movement towards increasing economic and political integration in Europe, all countries may be expected to become increasingly involved in this process, which must be regarded as affecting the body of European nations as a whole.

This development has major implications for public service-providing agencies in European countries, most of which have been used to operating within an ethnically homogeneous population. Police forces are no exception to this statement. A process of change is required to enable such agencies to function effectively, both as employers and providers of public services, in what is increasingly a multi-ethnic society. Training, of course, is one of the most important means of achieving the necessary adaptation to these new circumstances.

The aim of the present Council of Europe Meeting is to make a contribution to this process by bringing together persons currently engaged in planning and delivering training on these subjects to police officers. However, no systematic information existed previously on to what extent and in what ways such training had been introduced in the various countries of Europe. In order to obtain such information, it was therefore decided to carry out a small postal questionnaire survey of all Member States prior to the Meeting. This paper reports the results of that survey.

2.   The Survey

The survey constitutes an initial attempt to discover the extent and nature of the training being provided in the various countries of Europe to assist police officers to deal with matters concerning migrants and ethnic relations.

The aims of the survey have been:

(a)   to identify particular courses or other training initiatives that could be the subject of presentations at the Council of Europe Meeting;

(b)   to provide an overview of the current state of development of police training on these issues within Europe as a whole, as a general background to examination of particular initiatives at the meeting;

(c)   to provide an information base on current practice in individual
        Member States, that could assist the development of bilateral
        contacts and exchanges between those responsible for police
        training on these matters in individual States.

To achieve these aims, a short postal questionnaire was sent by the
Secretariat of the Council of Europe to more than a hundred agencies
in Member States which were believed to have a responsibility for the
training of police officers. These agencies included the relevant
government ministries in all Member States, together with national
police organisations and principal training establishments where these
were administered independently. In some Member States where
policing is organised regionally, questionnaires were sent to policing
authorities covering the main multi-ethnic residential areas. In those
Member States where there existed a public agency responsible for
matters concerning migrants and ethnic relations, a questionnaire was
sent to this body also.

Compiling a mailing list of all police training establishments in Member
States proved to be a major task. No complete list appeared to exist
previously, even for the EC countries. Valuable assistance was given
by the Police Study Centre in The Netherlands and by the Police Staff
College in Britain in compiling the mailing list. While it is hoped that the
mailing covered all relevant agencies at the national level in Member
States, resources did not permit the inclusion of all police authorities
and training institutions below this level. It should be recognised,
therefore, that there may be local or regional initiatives in some
countries which the survey may not have discovered.

Fifty-nine agencies had responded to the survey by the time of
preparation of this report. The Consultant, on behalf of the Council of
Europe, would like to thank all those who took the time and trouble to
produce the information that was requested.

The responses covered twenty of the Member States. A country-by-
country summary of the responses is provided in the *Appendix* to this
paper. Since not all of those contacted have replied, it cannot be
guaranteed that these responses represent a complete record of

current police training activity on these issues in Europe, even at national level. However, it seems reasonable to assume that those who did not respond either knew others were doing so on their behalf, or else had no responsibility for any activity of this kind. It is likely, therefore, that most (if not all) relevant police training activity in Europe has been identified.

3.   Summary of Findings of the Survey

The survey shows great variation among the Member States as regards the extent and manner of their response to issues concerning migrants and ethnic relations in police training. Some countries do not consider there to be a need to address these issues at all at the present time, while others plan to make adjustments across the police training system as a whole. Some provide training for specialist officers only, while others consider that all officers require training on these issues. Some have introduced specialised training courses in order to meet this need, while others have included the subjects in existing courses in one way or another.

Overall, the survey has found that most countries provide some degree of training for police officers on these subjects though it is often very limited in extent. The response from two countries stated that no such training was provided (and it must be remembered that several Member States did not respond to the survey at all). Some, moreover, appear to do so only with regard to entry control or in relation to general issues of human rights. The majority, however, appear to include some kind of specific instruction on immigration and migrant cultures - and perhaps also on prejudice and stereotypes - for some if not all officers. Very commonly this appears to consist of specific lessons which are included within a wider training programme, or within the component which deals with social and psychological issues.

Specialist training courses are less common, but also vary considerably in their format and in the officers who participate in them. A specialist training programme of some kind appeared to be offered in eight countries. However, this did not always consist of a course provided regularly within the police organisation. In France it consisted of a series of distinct events organised by the specialist training centre of the Police Nationale; while in Belgium it consisted of a training programme carried out by the independent Commissariat Royal not only for police but for staff in a variety of public service organisations.

In the four Nordic countries, on the other hand, a specialist course had been devised in each case at the national Police College for delivery on a regular basis to officers whose work brings them regularly into contact with "aliens". All the courses have ethnic relations as a major focus. The main Finnish course has a strong entry control component. but is complemented by a shorter seminar on ethnic relations which is incorporated into more general training. The Swedish course (DEFOIR project) was the first to be devised, but does not appear yet to be fully implemented. The Danish course was introduced in 1989, the Finnish course in 1990, and the Norwegian course in 1992.

In The Netherlands and the United Kingdom there are not only specialist courses, but also national strategies to address these issues both in training generally and by other means including recruitment of officers of migrant and minority backgrounds. In The Netherlands, the government has produced a formal "Positive Action Plan for Police and Ethnic Minorities", and training is the subject of one of the four "sub-projects" which have been established to implement the plan. This shows a very high public commitment by government and senior police officers to addressing these issues. The general aim is to transform the Dutch police service from a mono-ethnic into a multi-ethnic organisation, which will reflect the multi-ethnic nature of Dutch society. The main emphasis is on increasing recruitment from ethnic minorities, and on creating good staff relations. Alongside internal courses, such as the "Indian Summer Course" at the national Police Study Centre, outside organisations such as the Amsterdam-based Anne Frank Centre have also undertaken training programmes.

In the United Kingdom, the provision of training on these issues has a long history, especially at the Police Staff College at Bramshill. The current national strategy originates with a report on "Community and Race Relations Training for the Police", which was published in 1983 following Lord Scarman's Report on the Brixton Disorders of 1981. The report called for all police officers to receive training in these subjects, and for them to be integrated into courses at all levels. It recommended the establishment by the Home Office of an independent training support centre to assist with this process. The present "Specialist Support Unit" runs courses for trainers and training managers, and undertakes development work with training establishments throughout England and Wales. The aims of the training programme are to eliminate racial discrimination in both employment and service delivery, and to ensure that policing is sensitive to the needs of a multi-cultural society. A wide variety of initiatives have been undertaken by individual training schools. The implementation of the overall strategy is monitored and evaluated by the national Inspectorate of Constabulary.

4.   Reasons for Variation between Member States

There are many reasons for these variations in the response of Member States. The most obvious reason is the difference between Member States in the extent to which they have experienced immigration, and the period of time this process has been taking place. It is among those states with the larger and more long- established minorities of migrant origin that the principal initiatives have taken place. Other reasons for the variations include different national policies on immigration and on integration of groups of migrant origin. Differences in the role of the police or of particular police forces, and differences in the design and methods of training may also play a part. Overall, many factors are clearly involved, and it would seem a complex task to provide a full explanation and one which is obviously beyond the scope of this paper.

5. Stages of Development of Police Training Response

It seems possible, nonetheless, to distinguish five stages in the development of the response of police training to issues concerning migrants and ethnic relations. These are not always clear-cut, but the scheme may be useful in understanding the development of the training response in different Member States.

A. *No explicit coverage of issues in training*

The issues are not recognised as needing to be addressed, or are considered to be covered under broader headings such as "human rights" or "general psychology".

B. *Training provided for specialist officers*

The issues are recognised, but the training need is considered to be confined to officers responsible for entry control, or to specialist contact officers in areas of immigrant settlement.

C. *Specific topics included in general training courses*

It is recognised that the issues are relevant to all officers, but the response is solely to add the topics into existing training programmes. This usually takes the form of information-provision (e.g. about minority cultures), without addressing attitudes or skills.

D. *Specialist training provided for all officers*

It is recognised that the topics are sufficiently important for all officers to receive special training to bring the whole organisation to a new level not just of knowledge, but also of awareness and skill. This may take the form of free-standing courses, or special projects within general training programmes.

E. Issues integrated thematically into all training programmes

It is recognised that in a genuinely multi-ethnic organisation, these issues are central and must be built into the whole fabric of the organisation and its ongoing training programmes. Ideally, the issues have become so well integrated that specialist courses may no longer be required.

It is open to question whether all countries do need, or will in future need, to progress through these various stages. In any event, it must be acknowledged that the model is a simplified one. Nonetheless, the model may be useful both to identify the stage of development of the police training response in different Member States at the present time. It may also suggest directions in which the future development of training in particular countries may need to move as police authorities come to recognise the implications of the multi-ethnic dimension in European society.

For example, in Britain (as in The Netherlands) it is now recognised that Stage E needs to be the goal of training development programmes which are concerned with these issues. However, the work of the national Specialist Support Unit for training in this area (referred to earlier) is at present mainly engaged with the task of achieving Stage D. Police training in Britain has in fact already moved through the earlier stages, with courses for specialist officers being introduced during the 1970s (Stage B), and insertions into general training being made increasingly during the 1980s (Stage C). During the 1970s, however, the need for a more fundamental and extensive training response was not foreseen. Today, with hindsight, one can appreciate that it would have been desirable to put the present programmes into operation many years earlier. Perhaps, therefore, it may be possible for other Member States in Europe to learn from the British experience, and move more quickly to the level of training response that will be appropriate for policing Europe's increasingly multi-ethnic society.

6.   The Nature of the Problem for Police Training

One further aspect of this development process needs to be mentioned. The definition of the problem to be addressed tends to change as experience of tackling these issues in training progresses. In many countries the earliest initiatives emphasise mainly the need for knowledge about migrant and refugee groups - for *providing information* about their history and cultures. It is the groups themselves that are often seen as "the problem": creating problems for entry regulation perhaps, or being associated with particular forms of crime (e.g. drugs, juvenile gangs). As experience in this field increases, so it becomes recognised that "the problem" also lies in the majority or indigenous population, and in the agencies themselves. It is a problem not just of information, but also of attitudes that are prejudiced or ethnocentric, and of lack of skills to listen and communicate effectively where cultural differences are involved.

The more developed training programmes, therefore, recognise that it is the police themselves who need to change some of their attitudes and behaviour, and ensure that modern professional standards take account of the racial and cultural diversity of the communities that police officers serve. Such programmes therefore tend to focus more on *preventing discrimination* in police behaviour towards some sections of the public - whether it be discrimination resulting from personal prejudices and stereotypes, or whether it be unintended "institutional discrimination" resulting from outmoded and ethnocentric practices of a mono-ethnic past. Once again it may be said that, in Britain, it has taken many years for these lessons to become fully appreciated. In this respect too, by learning from previous experience it may be possible for other Member States to move more quickly to defining the "training problem" in a more accurate and effective way.

7.   Some Specific Initiatives

In addition to the various courses and other aspects of curriculum design that are discussed above, it may be useful to draw out examples of certain other kinds of specific initiatives that have been

155

taken in police training on these subjects in Member States. Five areas of initiative have been distinguished, but this list is not exhaustive, and not all initiatives are covered. Fuller details are included in the *Appendix*.

(a)   Training Materials

In several Member States, video programmes have been prepared or adapted for use in training on these subjects. Some provide audio-visual information about migrant or ethnic groups, or about particular problems or localities. Others are designed as "triggers" for exploring attitudes within the training group, or to assist in skills exercises concerned, for example, with multi- cultural communication. Video programmes of the latter kind have been produced in both the Netherlands and the UK.

Many different kinds of written materials have also been produced. Some simply provide detailed information on these subjects for students to read. In Britain, much use has been made in police training of extended "case-studies" based on real incidents, on which a wide-ranging programme of learning can be developed. Case-studies have been prepared, for example, on incidents of racial violence against minorities. In London's Metropolitan Police, a comprehensive handbook of information and exercises on these subjects has been produced to accompany the 20-week training programme for recruits.

(b)   Community Involvement

Learning through personal contact about the experiences and cultures of members of migrant and minority ethnic communities is rightly considered to be of great importance in a number of Member States. Visits to local community or religious centres, and talks from representatives of community groups or anti-racist organisations are used in many training establishments. Contact with young people of migrant origin through sport is also used, especially by the Berlin police. In London's Metropolitan Police College, a specialist "Community Involvement Unit" brings in members of local communities to meet recruits for two days of role-play and discussion. Similar events

have been organised for more experienced officers at community venues. At the Marseilles Training School, students undertake their own studies in the multi-ethnic city. In Britain, the "Specialist Support Unit" arranges for students to stay for a weekend with a minority ethnic family. These examples show some of the many different ways in which members of local communities may contribute to police training, and may of course gain in knowledge and understanding about the police in return.

(c)   Specialist Training Advisers

In most police training establishments, there are unlikely to be staff with specialist knowledge and skills for addressing these issues. Many training schools invite outside experts to give lectures, or to run short courses on their behalf (e.g. the programmes of the Police Nationale in France). Although the quality of these programmes may be high, they do not necessarily bring the issues into the mainstream programme of work of the training school. If the issues are to become an integral part of police training, then specialist staff or training advisers may need to be appointed. In the Netherlands and Britain, several police forces or training establishments have followed this practice, usually appointing someone with both expertise and a background in one of the minority ethnic communities. The appointment may be full-time or part-time. The British Home Office also has a full-time consultant who advises on these issues in police training, as well as in other areas of government responsibility.

(d)   Specialist Training Unit

Both the British and Dutch experience suggest that if Member States are serious about their commitment to address these issues in police training, then voluntary measures or local discretion are likely to produce slow progress at best. A clear policy commitment implemented through central direction or strategic planning would appear necessary if the police training systems of Member States are to respond at all rapidly to the increasingly multi-ethnic character of European society. Expert advice and support needs to be available at a national level for such a process to be effective. The Dutch Positive Action Plan adopts precisely this national approach, and has established a special "sub-project" to implement the training aspects. In Britain, the Home Office-sponsored "Specialist Support Unit" plays a similar developmental role. In both countries, the specialist unit is seen as a temporary device, whose task is equip the training schools to take responsibility for these issues themselves. Other Member States too may wish to consider the benefits of establishing specialist training units of this kind.

(e)   Tackling Racist and Xenophobic Violence

A special concern of both the European Parliament and the Council of Europe has been the rise of racist and xenophobic violence across Europe in recent years. This takes many forms, and its direction and extent varies between countries, but there are also themes and tendencies which are common to Europe as a whole. Responsibility for dealing with this problem lies substantially, though by no means solely, with the police. It is therefore an important subject for police training.

Although there was no direct question on this subject in the survey questionnaire, its relevance was mentioned in the covering letter. However, only three countries specifically mentioned this topic, and even in these cases it was unclear whether it was included in regular training. Specific initiatives included seminars on the subject in Germany (Hamburg, Berlin), and written and video-based training materials on the subject in Britain. It is of course accepted that the survey would not necessarily reveal all instances where this topic is covered in training. However, there was no sign that the topic is currently receiving the attention in police training that it would appear to deserve. This particular subject area, therefore, is surely one which would warrant further consideration among Member States.

Robin Oakley

Summary of responses
to questionnaire survey

This Appendix summarises the responses to the questionnaire survey on a country-by-country basis. In a few cases the responses are supplemented by information obtained from direct enquiries.

Each entry consists of two parts: (1) the agencies which responded to the survey; and (2) a summary of the activity reported. Activities which are asterisked are the subject of a presentation at the Meeting.

Austria

1.   Federal Ministry of the Interior (two departments); Federal Police.

2.   The topics of immigration and minorities, and of discrimination and xenophobic violence and intimidation. are included within initial and further training for all officers. The Vienna Police Training School has held several events on these subjects, including a seminar on multi-cultural issues in October 1991.

Belgium

1.   Gendarmerie; Ministry of Justice/Police Judiciale; Ministry of the Interior/Police Generale de Royaume; Commissariat Royal à la Politique des Immigrés.

2a.   In collaboration with the Ministry of the Interior, specialist training has been provided since 1990 by the *Commissariat Royal* to instructors and to police and gendarmerie officers in several regions including Brussels, and is being extended into other regions. It covers history of immigration, migrant cultures and religions, prejudice and stereotypes, and relationships with migrant groups (including local visits).

2b.   The *Gendarmerie* does not yet have a course specifically on the subject of multiculturalism, but links are made with this subject in other courses (e.g. on legislation, communication). In 1992, instructors trained by the Commissariat Royal are delivering a four-hour session to familiarise all operational personnel with these subjects, and attitude training will follow in 1993. A multi-disciplinary unit is being formed to study problems of youth and public order. A national campaign to recruit naturalised immigrants is also being planned.

2c.   The training of the *Judicial Police* includes coverage of racism within the subject of human rights. There is a plan to introduce a course on relations with migrants and ethnic groups in the near future.

Cyprus

1.   Ministry of Interior/National Police.

2.   The subject is not included as there are no groups of migrant origin in Cyprus.

Denmark

1.   National Police School.

2.   A four-week Specialist Course on "Police Activities towards and among Aliens" was introduced in 1989. The subjects of migrants, refugees, ethnic groups are included in the social studies components of basic and further training. Course evaluations show positive effects.

Finland

1.   National Police Academy, Espoo; National Police School, Tampere.

2.　　A two-week specialist "Aliens Course" (with follow-up course) was introduced in 1990. Its main focus is on entry controls and police relations with aliens. These topics are also included in general training. One/two day seminars on migrant issues and other cultures were introduced in 1991 into both basic and leadership training.

France

1.　　Ministry of Interior/Police nationale (Centre national d'études, Institut national de formation); Commission nationale consultative des droits de l'homme.

2a.　　The subjects are included in the training of officers of all ranks and specialisms in the *Police nationale*. Topics covered include the following: the law relating to foreigners, immigration, cultural differences and modes of communication, forms of social exclusion (intolerance, discrimination, racism), youth problems, and the ethics of a multi-cultural society. The newly created police training school at Marseilles has undertaken initiatives in this area, including involvement of representatives of local associations concerned with these issues in the training programme.

2b.　　Specialist courses on these subjects are provided at the *Centre national d'études et de formation de la police nationale*, at Gif-sur-Yvette. A variety of short courses have been held in recent years, using expert outside speakers. For example, a six-day awareness course on groups from the Maghreb, Black Africa and South-East Asia was organised in conjunction with L'Agence de developpement des relations interculturelles in late 1991. Summer Schools held in Marseille in 1990 and 1991, and at Gif in 1992, have focused on issues concerning young people of immigrant origin. A multi-agency study day on the same theme has been held for police officers and colleagues from other social agencies. Extensive documentation on these courses has been produced.

2c.   The "*Commission nationale consultative des droits de l'homme*", an advisory body to the Ministry of the Interior, does not undertake any training itself. However, as part of its work in tackling racism and xenophobia, it reviews the action taken in police training and makes recommendations accordingly.

Germany

1.   Police Academy, Munster; Bundeskriminalamt; Federal Interior Ministry/Federal Border Guards; State Interior Ministries: Hesse, (Berlin); State Police: Hamburg, Berlin; Berlin Ombudsman for Foreigners; Frankfurt Multi-Cultural Office

2a.   The major part of police training in Germany is conducted by the individual Land (State) police forces. Of the two *federal* police forces, the Federal Border Guards and the Bundeskriminalamt, neither undertakes specific training on issues of migrants and ethnic groups. The central Polizei-Fuhringsakademie at Munster, which is responsible for the training of senior officers, does not provide specific training on these subjects either, although during 1992 it organized two special seminars on the policing of violence against asylum seekers.

2b.   Some coverage has been introduced in police training at *Land level*. Issues such as prejudice and discrimination are included in the psychology component of training. In Hamburg, special seminars have been held on the problem of racist and xenophobic behaviour. Although in Hesse no special training provision is made on these subjects, the Multi-Cultural Office of Frankfurt reports that it is planning to offer training for police officers in the near future.

2c.   *Berlin* appears to be the Land which has been most active in this field. Although no specialist course is provided, there have been a number of activities on this subject. General training includes the following topics: prejudice, Berlin as a multi-cultural city, minority cultures and religions, and foreigners and crime. Training for both middle and higher-level officers includes a special component of "behaviour-training", which covers prejudice and communication towards foreigners. Strong emphasis is placed on "reciprocal contact", with visits to a mosque and football matches between trainees and Turkish youth. Special seminars have been held on foreigners in Berlin, asylum-seekers, and violence against minorities. The Berlin Ombudsman for Foreigners has spoken at these seminars. Separately from training, a police project "KICK-Sport against youth delinquency" is addressing similar issues.

Greece

1.   Ministry of Public Order/Hellenic Police.

2.   The subject is covered in a course on "International Public Law", and in a seminar on matters relating to control of aliens which is attended by all officers.

Hungary

1.   Ministry of Interior/Department for Refugees.

2.   Legal and social issues relating to migrants and refugees are taught in basic and further training, and to officers from the "aliens police". There is also a special project (no details provided).

Ireland

1.   Garda Siochana College.

2.   The topics of prejudice and discrimination against minority ethnic groups are included in the Social Psychology programme within initial training.

Italy

1.   Ministry of Interior/State Police.

2.   Training covers application of the regulations concerning foreigners, in the light of safeguarding human rights.

Luxembourg

1.   Ministry of Interior; Gendarmerie Grand-Ducal; Direction de la Police.

2.   Training does not include coverage of issues concerning relations with migrants and ethnic groups.

Netherlands

1.   National Police Coordinating Board; Police Study Centre, Warnsveld; Positive Action Plan: Training Sub-Project; Municipal Police: Rotterdam.

2a.   The main training initiative in this field in The Netherlands forms part of the "*National Positive Action Plan: Police and Ethnic Minorities*", published in 1988 by the Home Affairs Ministry, and implemented in 1989. The main objective of this plan is to increase recruitment of minorities and to transform the police from a mono-cultural to a multi-cultural organisation. The police forces of Amsterdam, Rotterdam, The Hague and some smaller police forces are currently participating in the project, which will finish in 1996.

2b.   A "*Training Sub-Project*" based at Rotterdam Police provides training for trainers, managers, personnel officers and others to support the implementation of the Plan. The main topics covered in training include: the need for positive action, dealing with resistance to positive action, cooperation among multi-cultural staff, cultural differences, relations with migrant communities.

2c.   Already before 1988 the subjects of migrants and ethnic relations had been included in training courses, especially in the four largest municipal forces. Also, the Home Affairs Ministry established a "Training, Advice and Course Team" (TACT) at the *Anne Frank Centre*, Amsterdam, which carried out a major police training programme in support of positive action between 1986 and 1990. Other organisations have also assisted, including a theatre production company which devised role-plays, and a company (CIRCON) which has produced videos for use in training on these subjects.

2d.   The *Police Study Centre* at Warnsveld provides training for senior managers on these subjects in a specialist "Indian Summer Course". This is designed to assist them to develop a "top-down" strategy for changing their organisation into a multi-cultural police force, in accordance with the Positive Action Plan.

Norway

1.   National Police College.

2.   A specialist course for officers in immigration control departments of local police forces was introduced in 1992: topics include migration, cultural differences, and cross-cultural communication. Some local police forces include matters concerning migrants and ethnic relations in their own programmes. Initial police training is being restructured along "higher education" lines, with a strong social science foundation: the study of migrant and ethnic issues will be incorporated within this.

Poland

1.   Ministry of Interior/Adviser for Migration.

2.   Issues relating to migrants and refugees in Poland are covered in senior officer training. A project to extend this provision is in preparation.

Portugal

1.   Ecole Superieure de Police; Institut National de Police et Sciences Criminelles/Judicial Police; National Republican Guard.

2.   In the Ecole Superieure, these issues are approached within the study of human rights and international law. The National Institute of Criminal Science includes the topics of immigration, prejudice and stereotypes within its training programme. On the whole, however, it is considered that circumstances in Portugal do not at the present time require these issues to be introduced into police training generally.

Spain

1.   Ministry of the Interior/National Police.

2.   The subjects are covered in general training as part of instruction on ethics and human rights received by all officers. Frontier control and problems of aliens and refugees are covered in courses run by the Centre for Development and Specialisation, and also in development courses at the Centre for Promotion. The seminar "Police in the European Community" studies social questions including racism, xenophobia and migration.

Sweden

1.   National Police College; Ombudsman Against Discrimination.

2.   A specialist training programme (DEFOIR: Democracy, Human Rights and Inter-Ethnic Relations) has been developed but not yet fully implemented. Understanding of foreign cultures is included in basic training. Special seminars are also arranged. Police training generally is under review. The Swedish Ombudsman Against Discrimination has given talks to police officers.

Switzerland

1.   Institute Suisse de Police; Conference des Commandants des Polices Cantonales; Federal Aliens Office.

2.   Training on control of foreigners and policy relating to refugees and asylum-seekers is given to officers with specialist responsibilities for these matters. The subject is also included in the pre-entry training for police candidates. Most police training is carried out by autonomous cantonal police services (not contacted individually in this survey). The canton of Zug is planning a seminar in 1993 on police relations with foreigners (including topics of prejudice, communication, etc.).

United Kingdom

1.   Home Office; Association of Chief Police Officers (England & Wales, Scotland); Police Staff College, Bramshill; Scottish Police College; Central Planning and Training Unit, Harrogate; Specialist Support Unit, Turvey; individual police forces - Derbyshire, Manchester, Metropolitan/London (Equal Opportunities Unit, Recruit Training School), West Midlands, West Yorkshire; Commission for Racial Equality.

2a.   Training on these issues forms part of a *national strategy* to promote equal opportunities in employment in the police, and to improve relationships between the police and minority ethnic communities. The Home Office, which is responsible for overall training policy, sponsors various initiatives in this field. Special emphasis is placed on tackling the problem of racial attacks and harassment, and a training video has been produced. The national Inspectorate of Constabulary has a senior police officer responsible for overseeing implementation of policy on these issues.

2b.   An independent "*Specialist Support Unit*", established by the Home Office in 1989, assists police training schools to integrate "community and race relations" issues into their training curricula, and runs a six-week training course for instructors on this subject. This includes a weekend spent in the home of a minority ethnic family. Courses are also run for managers who are responsible for developing training on these subjects. A four-phase training programme on these issues to be delivered to police officers throughout the country has been planned and is in process of implementation. The Commission for Racial Equality is represented on the Unit's management board.

2c.   The *Police Staff College* at Bramshill runs specialist courses on "Police and Visible Minorities" and "Equal Opportunities", and also includes these issues in its management training courses. The national Central Planning and Training Unit, which is mainly concerned with training up to Inspector rank, integrates these issues throughout its training programmes and is currently developing this process further.

2d.   London's *Metropolitan Police* have given these issues a high profile since the early 1980s. Training initiatives are coordinated by the Equal Opportunities Unit. A programme of "Fair Treatment Training" for trainers and managers has been in operation since early 1990, with emphasis on combatting racial and other forms of discrimination in employment. At the Metropolitan Police College at Hendon, the Recruit Training School deals with these issues both as specialist topics and by linking them into other subjects in the basic training curriculum. In addition, the "Reciprocal Training Scheme" enables members of local community groups to become involved in training activities. A comprehensive handbook giving information about legislation, migration and minority communities in London accompanies the course.

2e.   The training schools of *other police forces* have also undertaken many initiatives, as well as integrating these subjects into general training. The following are examples. Derbyshire police run a one-week "National Race Relations Course", and a four-week course for specialist "Community Liaison Officers". West Yorkshire police training school has a officer with special responsibility for these issues, and engages outside contributors from local communities to help deliver training on them. West Midlands police have developed a special training package based on an incident of racial violence which occurred locally; they also provide access training for potential ethnic minority recruits. Northumbria police appointed a civilian Race Relations Adviser of Asian background to assist with training on these subjects.

2f.   Police training in *Scotland* is organised independently of England and Wales. At the Scottish Police College, initial training includes coverage of immigration, racism, discrimination, and minority cultures and religions. Further training courses also include some coverage of ethnic relations. Individual police forces also provide training for officers working in local areas with substantial minority ethnic populations, and in some cases use civilian race relations specialists to assist with such training.

Robin Oakley

List of participants

Chairman

M. Bertrand MAIN, Chef du Bureau de l'Action sociale, culturelle et du cadre de vie, Direction de la population et des migrations, ministère des Affaires sociales et de l'Intégration, 1 place de Fontenoy, 75700 Paris, FRANCE

Project organisers

M. Daniel BELLET, Directeur, Centre national d'études et de formation de la Police nationale, ministère de l'Intérieur, Plateau du Moulon, 91192 Gif-sur-Yvette Cedex, *FRANCE*

M. Houssein BOUKHRISS, Commissariat royal à la politique des Immigrés, Résidence Palace, 155 rue de la Loi, 1040-Bruxelles, *BELGIUM*

Mr Albert BUITENHUIS, Police Study Centre, Rijkstraatweg 127, 7231 AD Warnsveld, *NETHERLANDS*

Mr Erkki ELLONEN, Police School, PL 25, 33501 Tampere, *FINLAND*

Mr Norman GREENHILL, Police Staff College, Bramshill House, Bramshill, Basingstoke RG27 0JW, Hampshire, *UNITED KINGDOM*

Mr Vidar HALVORSEN, Police College, P.O. Box 5027, Majorstua, 0301 Oslo, *NORWAY*

Mr Jan van KOOTEN, Anne Frank Centre, P.O. Box 730, 1000 AS Amsterdam, *NETHERLANDS*

Mr Eckhardt LAZAI, Berlin Police Department, Radelandstrasse 21, 1000 Berlin 20, *GERMANY*

Mr Jerome MACK, Specialist Support Unit, Home Office, Queen Anne's Gate, London SW1H 9AT, *UNITED KINGDOM*

Mr John David MOORE, HM Inspectorate of Constabulary, Home Office, Queen Anne's Gate, London SW1H 9AT, *UNITED KINGDOM*

Mr Türker SOUKKAN, Swedish National Police College, Sörentorp, 171 92 Solna, *SWEDEN*

Mr Arne THOMSEN, Danish Police College, Artillerivej 55, 2300 Copenhagen S, *DENMARK*

Other participants

Belgium: M. Francesco SANT'ANGELO, Commissariat royal à la politique des Immigrés, Résidence Palace, 155 rue de la Loi, 1040 Bruxelles, BELGIUM

Mme Eliane DEPROOST, Conseiller, Commissariat royal à la politique des Immigrés, Résidence Palace, 155 rue de la Loi, 1040 Bruxelles, BELGIUM

Bulgaria: M. Evgeni STOYANOV PALYOV, Service juridique, ministère de l'Intérieur, 29 rue du 6 septembre, 1000 Sofia, BULGARIA

Germany: Mrs Bettina FRANZKE, Office for Multicultural Affairs, Barckhausstr. 1-3, 6000 Frankfurt, GERMANY

Greece: Mr Elias VLACHOVIANNIS, Police Major, Ministry of Public Order, 185-187 Socratous Street, Kallithea-Athens, GREECE

Mr Dimitrios VOUKALIS, Professor, 35 28eme Otcobziou Street, Brilissia, Athens, GREECE

Italy: Dr. Gaetano TORNATORE, Ministry of the Interior, Departimento P.S., Servizio Stranieri, Rome, ITALIA

Dr Antonio TOZZI, Ministry of the Interior, Dir della Scuola di Polizia di Frontiera di Duino (TS), Via della Cernizza N° 67/B, Duino (TS), ITALIA

Portugal: M. Fernando M. AFONSO DE ALMEIDA, Directeur de l'Ecole supérieure de Police, Rua 10 de Maio N°3, 1300 Lisboa, PORTUGAL

Mme Maria Helena BASTOS MARTINS, Inspecteur du Service d'étrangers et frontières Rua Conselheiro José Silvestre Ribeiro N° 4, 1600 Lisboa, PORTUGAL

Federation of Russia: Mr Andrew V. NESTEROV, Senior Lecturer, Police Academy of Russia, 26-1-52 Academica Skriabina Street, 109378 Moscow, FEDERATION OF RUSSIA

Slovenia: Mr Bogdan STARE, Head of Department for Foreigners, Ministry for Internal Affairs, Stefanova 2, 61000 Ljubljana, SLOVENIA

Spain: Mr José A. MARCOS PINEIRO, Inspector, JEFE, Centro de promocion de la Division de formacion y perfeccionamiento de la policia, Plaza de Carabanchel N° 5, 28025 Madrid, SPAIN

M. Antonio P. GOMEZ VAZQUEZ, Inspecteur, JEFE, Comisaria General de documentacion, Sericio de Fronteras y Extranjeros, C/ General Pardinas N° 90, 28006 Madrid, SPAIN

Sweden: Mr Nils ERIKSSON, Swedish National Police College, Sörentorp, 171 92 Solna, SWEDEN

Switzerland: M. Serge HAUSMANN, Chef du Bureau des habitants et de la police des étrangers de la Commune de Morges, 1110 Morges, SWITZERLAND

United Kingdom: Mr Trevor HALL, Community Relations Consultant, I Division, Home Office, Queen Anne's Gate, London SW1H 9AT, UNITED KINGDOM

Consultant

Dr Robin OAKLEY, 20A Boscastle Road, London NW5 1EG, UNITED KINGDOM

Sales agents for publications of the Council of Europe
Agents de vente des publications du Conseil de l'Europe

AUSTRALIA/AUSTRALIE
Hunter publications, 58A, Gipps Street
AUS-3066 COLLINGWOOD, Victoria
Fax: (61) 34 19 71 54

AUSTRIA/AUTRICHE
Gerold und Co., Graben 31
A-1011 WIEN 1
Fax: (43) 1512 47 31 29

BELGIUM/BELGIQUE
La Librairie européenne SA
50, avenue A. Jonnart
B-1200 BRUXELLES 20
Fax: (32) 27 35 08 60

Jean de Lannoy
202, avenue du Roi
B-1060 BRUXELLES
Fax: (32) 25 38 08 41

CANADA
Renouf Publishing Company Limited
1294 Algoma Road
CDN-OTTAWA ONT K1B 3W8
Fax: (1) 613 741 54 39

DENMARK/DANEMARK
Munksgaard
PO Box 2148
DK-1016 KØBENHAVN K
Fax: (45) 33 12 93 87

FINLAND/FINLANDE
Akateeminen Kirjakauppa
Keskuskatu 1, PO Box 218
SF-00381 HELSINKI
Fax: (358) 01 21 44 35

GERMANY/ALLEMAGNE
UNO Verlag
Poppelsdorfer Allee 55
D-53115 BONN
Fax: (49) 228 21 74 92

GREECE/GRÈCE
Librairie Kauffmann
Mavrokordatou 9, GR-ATHINAI 106 78
Fax: (30) 13 83 03 20

HUNGARY/HONGRIE
Euro Info Service
Magyarorszag
Margitsziget (Európa Ház),
H-1138 BUDAPEST
Fax: (36) 1 111 62 16

IRELAND/IRLANDE
Government Stationery Office
4-5 Harcourt Road, IRL-DUBLIN 2
Fax: (353) 14 75 27 60

ISRAEL/ISRAËL
ROY International
PO Box 13056
IL-61130 TEL AVIV
Fax: (972) 3 546 1442

ITALY/ITALIE
Libreria Commissionaria Sansoni
Via Duca di Calabria, 1/1
Casella Postale 552, I-50125 FIRENZE
Fax: (39) 55 64 12 57

MALTA/MALTE
L. Sapienza & Sons Ltd
26 Republic Street
PO Box 36
VALLETTA CMR 01
Fax: (356) 246 182

NETHERLANDS/PAYS-BAS
InOr-publikaties, PO Box 202
NL-7480 AE HAAKSBERGEN
Fax: (31) 542 72 92 96

NORWAY/NORVÈGE
Akademika, A/S Universitetsbokhandel
PO Box 84, Blindern
N-0314 OSLO
Fax: (47) 22 85 30 53

PORTUGAL
Livraria Portugal, Rua do Carmo, 70
P-1200 LISBOA
Fax: (351) 13 47 02 64

SPAIN/ESPAGNE
Mundi-Prensa Libros SA
Castelló 37, E-28001 MADRID
Fax: (34) 15 75 39 98

Llibreria de la Generalitat
Rambla dels Estudis, 118
E-08002 BARCELONA
Fax: (34) 34 12 18 54

SWEDEN/SUÈDE
Aktiebolaget CE Fritzes
Regeringsgatan 12, Box 163 56
S-10327 STOCKHOLM
Fax: (46) 821 43 83

SWITZERLAND/SUISSE
Buchhandlung Heinimann & Co.
Kirchgasse 17, CH-8001 ZÜRICH
Fax: (41) 12 51 14 81

BERSY
Route du Manège 60, CP 4040
CH-1950 SION 4
Fax: (41) 27 31 73 32

TURKEY/TURQUIE
Yab-Yay Yayimcilik Sanayi Dagitim Tic Ltd
Barbaros Bulvari 61 Kat 3 Daire 3
Besiktas, TR-ISTANBUL

UNITED KINGDOM/ROYAUME-UNI
HMSO, Agency Section
51 Nine Elms Lane
GB-LONDON SW8 5DR
Fax: (44) 171 873 82 00

UNITED STATES and CANADA/
ÉTATS-UNIS et CANADA
Manhattan Publishing Company
468 Albany Post Road
PO Box 850
CROTON-ON-HUDSON, NY 10520, USA
Fax: (1) 914 271 58 56

STRASBOURG
Librairie Kléber
Palais de l'Europe
F-67075 STRASBOURG Cedex
Fax: (33) 88 52 91 21

Council of Europe Publishing/Editions du Conseil de l'Europe
Council of Europe/Conseil de l'Europe
F-67075 Strasbourg Cedex
Tel. (33) 88 41 25 81 - Fax (33) 88 41 27 80